Prince OF CRIME

John Morgan

STEIN AND DAY / *Publishers*/ New York

First published in the United States of America in 1985
Copyright © 1985 by John Morgan
All rights reserved, Stein and Day, Incorporated
Designed by Louis A. Ditizio
Printed in the United States of America
STEIN AND DAY/*Publishers*
Scarborough House
Briarcliff Manor, N.Y. 10510

Library of Congress Cataloging in Publication Data

Morgan, John, 1929-
  Prince of crime.

  Bibliography: p.
  Includes index.
    1. Humphreys, Murray.   2. Crime and criminals—
Illinois—Chicago—Bibliography.   3. Gangs—Illinois—
Chicago—History.   I. Title.
HV6248.H77M67   1985   364.1'092'4   [B]   85-40248
ISBN 0-8128-3050-4

For Aled, with love
on his twenty-first birthday

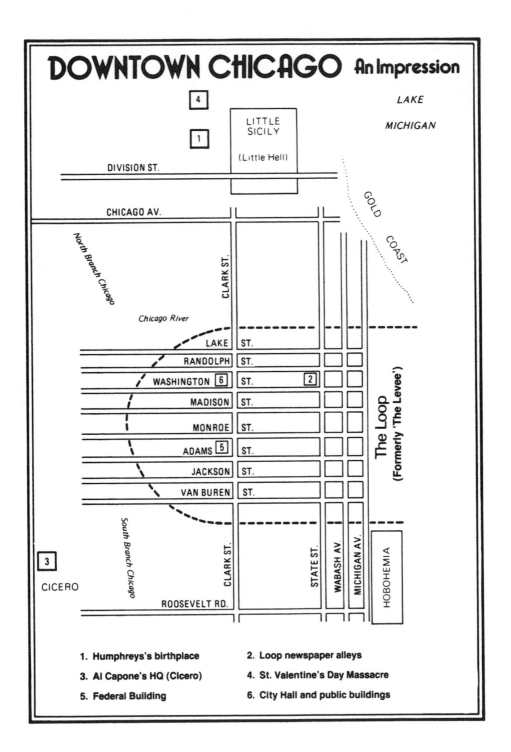

DOWNTOWN CHICAGO An Impression

LAKE

MICHIGAN

4

1

LITTLE
SICILY

(Little Hell)

DIVISION ST.

GOLD COAST

CHICAGO AV.

North Branch Chicago

CLARK ST.

Chicago River

LAKE ST.

RANDOLPH ST.

WASHINGTON 6 ST. 2

MADISON ST.

MONROE ST.

ADAMS 5 ST.

JACKSON ST.

VAN BUREN ST.

The Loop
(Formerly 'The Levee')

South Branch Chicago

3

CICERO

CLARK ST.

STATE ST.

WABASH AV.

MICHIGAN AV.

HOBOHEMIA

ROOSEVELT RD.

1. Humphreys's birthplace

2. Loop newspaper alleys

3. Al Capone's HQ (Cicero)

4. St. Valentine's Day Massacre

5. Federal Building

6. City Hall and public buildings

Contents

List of Illustrations

Foreword

The quest for Llewelyn (Murray) Humphreys began in the
desire to make a television documentary film about a vaguely
known gangster of Welsh origin who was known to have been a
colleague of Al Capone's. Only when we began making inquiries in Chicago did we discover that the man was more
important than any histories of his epoch had proposed. Therefore, this biography has its origins in the research done in the
United States by my colleagues, Huw Davies, the Director of
Programs at HTV Wales, and the documentary film's director,
Don Llewelyn. As important as their contribution has been the
help given me by Karen May of Chicago, particularly in building up the portrait of Humphreys from that city's newspapers
during the years of his success. The film we made is entitled *It
Takes a Crooked Man*. However, all three of my colleagues are
absolved from responsibility: first for my choosing to present
Humphreys as a man who achieved a potent form of the American Dream, secondly for those elements incorporated in the
biography that depend on other reporting I have done from the
United States, and lastly for my maturing view of that society.

However, I am indebted to them for introducing me to the
important witnesses to the life of Humphreys. His daughter,
Llewella, entertained us generously in Oklahoma; we did our
best to respond in Wales. Her conversation is enchanting, her
affection for her parents undimmed. Without her our film, as
this book, could not have possessed whatever insights each may
offer. The testimony of William Roemer, the FBI agent who
pursued Humphreys long and who knew him well, invaluably
supported an interpretation of the gangster's career that might
have seemed high-flown: to wit, that the Welshman's talent was

9

vital to the triumphs of the Outfit or Syndicate or Mob, as the Chicago hoods are variously entitled. The newspaper columnist Art Petaque was also an important and entertaining corroborator.

I am grateful to HTV Wales for granting permission to quote from my recorded conversation with Llewella Humphreys—her maiden name—with Mr. Roemer and Mr. Petaque, and for the freedom to reproduce the Humphreys's pictures from the documentary film. Those authors whose works I found most useful in understanding a gangster who was so anxious to keep out of sight are listed in the bibliography. I have a debt also to the Chicago newspapers and to the publications of the Chicago Crime Commission. In trying to portray a man who willfully eschewed biography I needed all the help available, but realize that there remains so much more that he alone knew about American crime, law, business, trade unions, cinema, and politics. Humphreys did not much distinguish between such various elements in his society. He was seldom wrong.

June 1985

1

Humphreys: the great unknown gangster

Our interest's on the dangerous edge of things.
The honest thief, the tender murderer,
The superstitious atheist, demirep
That loves and saves her soul in new French books—
We watch while these in equilibrium keep
The giddy line midway: one step aside
They're classed and done with.
—Robert Browning

Murray Humphreys, Public Enemy Number One, heir
to Scarface Al Capone's power, the brains of the so-
called Syndicate and the directing agent behind the
musclemen and killers who have dominated numerous
unions and so-called trade associations.
—Court Indictment, Chicago, June 1933

The politician as gangster is a familiar figure in history; the
gangster as politician is more unusual. Llewelyn Morris "Murray" Humphreys is as brilliant an example of the second cate-
gory as any society could wish not to find. He introduced crime
into the bloodstream of American society. In the opinion of
those who pursued him for forty years—whether police, the FBI,
prosecuting lawyers, judges, or murderous rivals—this hand-

some, elegant, articulate, and artistic son of Welsh-speaking immigrants to Chicago was an incomparable foe. His intellect graced his bombing, grunting, and psychopathic Mafioso colleagues and his reckless Irish killer enemies; so much so that he made the gangster a part of government.

One FBI agent who pursued him for eight years at the particular behest of Attorney General Robert Kennedy—although knowing that Humphreys was a murderer, an acid-thrower, an intimidator, and a corrupter of judges and politicians, and having met him fifty times—was beguiled by his charm and certainly moved at the news of the gangster's death. Humphreys died in 1965 at the age of sixty-six—of "unnatural causes, a heart attack," as the Chicago wit Mike Royko put it in a savage obituary. The Welshman, in a long career, had survived all the bloody battles that had seen most of his friends and enemies shot down. He was a prodigy in the criminal battles of the poor in Chicago before Prohibition. He rose to riches through that moralistic spasm and bootleg liquor, and, when it was done, he transformed crime in the United States from brutal hooliganism into a force that was to sway business and national affairs. NO GANGSTER WAS MORE BOLD ran a banner headline when he died.

Immediately the question arises: if Humphreys was so powerful, if he exercised so important a role in twentieth-century American life, why is he so little known? The answer is contingent on several other answers that have much to do with the usual difficulty in offering any account of the Outfit. Most people in public life cherish secrecy: the gangster has better reason even than the politician or the company director or trade union leader to keep his affairs to himself. Maintaining accounts is not wise; keeping minutes of meetings is not to be recommended. Even the threat of sudden death cannot always guarantee loyalty and trust. Thus, in piecing together an account of the behavior of mobsters—even of the stature and renown of Capone's Outfit or Syndicate—there are contradictions about dates, times, the structure of organization, meeting places, the ownership of brothels, saloons, and gambling establishments, whether to do with horse racing, dogs, lotteries or, later, after Humphreys' triumph in Las Vegas, slot machines and spinning wheels. Evidence at trials, eyewitness accounts, reminiscences of public officials—each for different reasons can be unreliable. Which politician would boast of his connection?

Historians dealing with the politician as gangster have less difficulty. In the European medieval period, behavior that in later epochs would be regarded as gangsterism was held to be the normal conduct of the state. The observation that political power comes out of the barrel of a gun might have been made by the twentieth-century Chinese leader Mao Tse-tung but would have seemed a tedious cliché to combatants in Britain's Wars of the Roses—or indeed to any European king or baron in the years before the Enlightenment. Such periods are well-documented. Similarly, in the present century the rise to power and its employment by Hitler, Stalin, and Mussolini is set down in authenticated records. When Bertolt Brecht wrote his extended metaphor of the Nazi German triumph in terms of Al Capone and Chicago in *The Resistible Rise of Arturo Ui,* he could be certain of his account of Hitler, less so of the true history of the Outfit. Brecht had not been to America when he wrote the play; such was the power of the Outfit's legend. Moreover, Brecht had never heard of Humphreys.

To the biographer's general difficulty is added Humphreys's unique sensitivity. He was Browning's "honest thief, tender murderer." He eschewed fame. Had he chosen, when the authorities declared him the most important gangster after Capone, to give press conferences like Capone and be available to foreigners for approbation, he would have been treated as one of the most famous people in the United States. For that reason he retreated—not from power but from the limelight. His daughter suggested to me that he decided to do so because he thought it was stupid for the Outfit to be in the public eye. He was hard on colleagues who paraded their wealth. Many who were ostentatious were killed. Others went to jail for offenses that could have been obscured but for vainglory. This would suggest that his concern was merely practical. Publicity was bad for business and therefore should be avoided.

Since it was one of Humphreys's serious achievements that he moved the Outfit's money into respectable American corporations once Prohibition was abolished in the early thirties, his distaste for publicity was fruitful. The principal engines of the most powerful economy in the world would not like it known that Humphreys was laundering money from the criminal world to sustain them. (His enthusiasm for laundries and his role in fixing both owners and unions was vital in his career: he *invented* the concept of laundering money.) The cogency of his analysis might suggest that it sprang from an intellectual gift alone. I suspect there was even more to it than that.

Let us imagine what it must have been like to be Humphreys. He was to be honored among his peers in time as the "brainy hood," the "Einstein," "Mr. Moneybags," and be flattered by the compliments of the Senate as the most grave of gangsters, a far more serious enemy than the Mafia. He had known the Colosimos, O'Banions, Capones, Lombardos, Yules, all the world-famous hoods—and had seen them shot or jailed. He had bought judges and lawyers and presidents' campaign managers. He had strolled around the White House, had thrown bombs at a president's father, had arranged the assassination of a Chicago mayor standing alongside President Roosevelt. He had bribed a state legislature to make gambling legal. He had so arranged things that the most powerful film studios in the world, in Hollywood, worked under his intimidation; he had seen his colleagues in that enterprise go to jail while he himself was not even arrested. He had tutored the gangsters to plead the Fifth Amendment when interrogated by the Senate and been so pleased by his invention that he hand-carpentered the plea in his study in a house he built himself in Oklahoma.

There were other brilliant legal coups; there were also horrible murders he committed or caused to be committed. Undoubtedly he was angry that in the sixties his old rival and colleague Joe Kennedy could not prevent his children, President John and Attorney General Robert, from harassing the Outfit: assassination was, as ever, the outcome. But even in the Outfit's dealings with the Kennedys, he was urging less publicity, trying to restrain those—like his protégé Sam Giancana—who sought the headlines by exchanging a mistress with President Kennedy. Humphreys arranged the transfer; Giancana was murdered; Humphreys died of a heart attack.

Can it therefore be only a concern for the welfare of the Outfit that persuaded Humphreys to step back and manipulate the thugs and hooligans? I suggest that he may have comprehended Nietzsche's idea of the great man, of that power transcending the apparatus of power. People who knew Humphreys propose that he should have been a senator, so eloquent was he, so shrewd, so studious of world affairs. What a shame that he left school at the age of seven and mixed with the precocious hoodlums in the Loop in Chicago! His clever mother and idle but affable father would have brought with them from Wales the idea that politics is fun, a game for the bright—but also a means whereby the poor get even.

All this must be part of the answer to the question: why is Humphreys the unknown gangster? He would allow only his surname to be placed on his tomb in Oklahoma, so acute was his fastidiousness. He could carry a joke into eternity, yet his jokes (and many became celebrated) were never his undoing. Nothing was his undoing. So, while it is true that the standard histories of crime and politics in the United States in his great days from 1928 to 1965 carry scarcely a reference to Humphreys, research into the day-to-day murders and the critical court and Senate hearings reveal that there was one figure ever present—or nearby, advising. Moreover, conversations with the FBI or Chicago journalists or shy politicians sustain the view that here was the most serious American gangster of them all.

From the evidence of the FBI, Chicago journalists and politicians and bondsmen and, especially, his daughter—each regarded him as the most important gangster. Further, those like Nitti, Accardo, Giancana, and the others in the Mafia who have been the subject of world attention, were placed in their jobs by Humphreys. At the Mob's board meetings, his was the decisive voice. If he became, as his daughter attests, weary of the game, he maintained among his acquaintances until the end a courtesy none of the animals he mixed with could pretend to.

When FBI agent William Roemer was charged by the Kennedys to find a way of arresting Humphreys, his first meeting with Humphreys took an odd form. Mr. Roemer said he was upset that his children were being harassed by the Outfit. Humphreys expressed surprise and regret at this. He walked away across the Chicago River—this was 1958. A few days later he returned to the FBI agent and assured him that his children would not be harassed any more—some fool had made a mistake, and would not make the same mistake again.

Other anecdotes about Humphreys's good manners are more bizarre. For example, when Humphreys and the famous murderer Sam "Golf Bag" Hunt were with some rich Chicagoan sportsmen after a day at the races in 1929, Humphreys, when Golf Bag placed his false teeth in Humphreys's spaghetti, was regarded as being a real gentler an because he did not wing Golf Bag with his surprisingly small revolver. (I have held it in my hand.) Legend has it that all Humphreys said was, "Keep your teeth to yourself, Sam"—a very Welsh locution.

Once the suggestion was made that Humphreys had *chosen* the shadows, for however practical or mischievous a reason, then the evidence became available. Because historians had concentrated on the men who chose or were forced into the limelight, Humphreys became a footnote at most. The newspapers in Chicago, considered from a different point, offered sufficient evidence to sustain the thesis that Humphreys really is the key to understanding how a group that personified the Hobbesian appraisal of human and political life as "nasty, brutish and short" could have helped to shape one of the two most powerful societies in the world.

Ascribing anyone's talent or genius is a dubious business. The temptation is strong for a Welshman to suggest that Humphreys, in his manipulation of the most powerful gang of criminals the twentieth century has seen—apart from formal political forces like Hitler's or Stalin's—was playing a game familiar to his compatriots. It has been expressed in their favorite sport of rugby football, where the star is the outside-half or three-quarter. He is usually small and alert and can dance through the lunges of huge men. The tradition is strong. To dance as he did through the bullets and bombs, avoiding the carnage while helping, in his apprentice days, to organize it, might sustain a sentimental thesis. Like David Lloyd George, whose speeches his father heard when young, he clearly had that rare political talent to see first what was on the other side of the hill, even if he put the gift to perverse uses.

Before he died he visited his father's birthplace in Wales, a cottage grandly named *Y Castell* (the Castle). He took with him his first wife and his second wife. He filmed his travels, which is how I came to learn that he was a cineaste who had made, edited, and created the soundtracks for substantial documentaries. A man so various that he seemed to be not one but all mankind's epitome, perhaps. Nevertheless, what distinguished him from other political geniuses of his time is that he did shoot people with his own gun. In considering his career it is easy to be distracted—by his exploitation of a materialist society and by his view that the respectable in America were corrupt—from the fact that for all that Humphreys is unknown, his achievement was majestic and sinister.

He did not need to read Niccolò Machiavelli's classic handbook for the aspiring ruler, *The Prince*. It could not have taught him anything. But no warrior springs fully armed from the womb. Where did Humphreys come from? From what kind of Welsh family background? What was the Chicago in which he grew into gangsterdom and wealth? Each formed him.

2

The Wales the Humphreys left behind

The future King Henry VII commanded his train to halt at a Welsh shepherd's cottage on the banks of the River Severn in the year 1485 because of the repute in which the humble man was held as a prophet. He asked him as to his future. "*Arglwydd* (Lord)," the Welshman replied, "you will fight great battles and you will win." When the King had departed the shepherd's wife said: "Why be so foolish as to prophesy for the King?" "Wife," said the Welshman, "if I am right, the King will reward me. If I am wrong, he will be dead."
> —Montgomery legend, also ascribed to the poet Dafydd Llwyd ap Llywelyn of Matharfarn.

A happy band on the hill slope
Were we that day, in high hope,
All at stretch and in good heart,
Resolute to play our part
With doughty deeds in winning fame
In men's mouths for Owain's name.
And there before the fray began,
In keen debate our talk ran
What part of profit each should gain
In booty when the foe was slain;
And ere a foeman hove in sight
Each averred, come what might,
Never yielding, he'd be found
Standing gloriously his ground.
> —*The Battle of Waun Gaseg,*
> Llywelyn ab y Moel (d. 1440)

The great, clever gangster's parents, Brian and Ann, were born within ten miles of one another. The Humphreys's small farmhouse, more a cottage, stands on a low hill at Carno. When I arrived in the yard of the gangster's father's home, a black lamb ran from the ruined barn. Legend has it that a small fort once stood on the ground of *Y Castell*—some Celtic or Roman stronghold commanding a view of the valley and the territory toward England. The fact of the name carried weight with the family. While expatriates in poverty in Chicago, the Humphreys would talk of the Castle and the time when they would once more occupy so grand a manor. Being born on the crown of hills in a cottage with such a title can, not unreasonably, create enduring romantic confusions.

Most people in the place at that time spoke Welsh, the oldest living European language. The Humphreys, like a majority of their two million compatriots, also spoke English, so that when they went to Chicago they did not share the language problems of the Poles, Germans, Italians, and Swedes they found themselves among. Evan Humphreys spent some of his time as a cattle drover, guiding the animals from Carno to Llanidloes and beyond, to England. The principal market was at Shrewsbury. It was there that the verb "to welsh" is held to have its origins. The English argue that it was the cunning, cheating behavior of the Welsh drovers that led to the word's connotation. In turn, the Welsh allege that the verb means "to cheat the Welsh."

The culture that the Humphreys took with them to the United States was bewildering. One element was the powerful language of the Bible: every home had a large copy of the good book in the Welsh language. In Welsh its eloquence has an even more apocalyptic force.

THE QUIET OF the Welsh countryside is misleading. It was not, in the youth of the gangster's parents, as agricultural as it is now. The lead mines were busy attracting migrant labor from England and Ireland. But the lead mines went into decline in the 1880s; the demand for wool fell; agriculture went into a slump. What future was there for young people? Where should they look for a bright prospect?

Throughout the Welsh countryside the question was being asked—and usually answered by a migration within Wales, to the coalfields and the steel and tinplate works of South and Southwest Wales. Here there was taking place one of the historic industrial expansions. The Humphreys decided to look westward and to emigrate across the Atlantic. They did not have the same pressure to go to the United States as, say, the Irish or Italians. Wales, strangely, did not suffer a net migration of people toward the end of the century; indeed, the population remained constant in numbers. But to the United States they went.

To think of going to the United States from what were landlocked small communities was not odd. The exporting of goods from small factories made the exotic foreign placenames familiar. The port of Barmouth nearby had trafficked across the Atlantic for centuries. The Humphreys may not have been aware that more Welshmen signed the Declaration of Independence than any other people, or that great universities had been founded by compatriots, or that—as some historians had it—Prince Madoc had discovered the New World long before Christopher Columbus. But if all this scholarship was unfamiliar, they were capable of reading the advertisements in the local press telling when ships were leaving and how much a passage to a new life cost. The Welsh press offered several routes. The most popular ports of embarkation were Liverpool and Bristol. Living where they did, the Humphreys chose Liverpool even though it was crowded with even-more-impoverished Irish.

Strong Welsh communities existed in America, especially in Pennsylvania and Ohio. Welsh-language papers were published; chapels flourished, their ministers arguing against drink—there were Welsh saloons. Most of these immigrants worked in the steel, tinplate, and iron factories and in the coal mines, often as managers. The Humphreys chose to ignore these established centers and make directly for Chicago on Lake Michigan, the fresh crossroads and market of the new enormous nation.

3

The Chicago they found

Chicago is the second American city, the fifth German
city, the third Swedish, the second Polish. . . .
—G. W. Steevens, 1895

Chicago was corrupted the day the first Anglo-Saxon
gave the first bottle of whisky to a Red Indian.
—Nelson Algren

Several European nations believe, with reason, that the United
States belongs to them. The English believe they have the
strongest claim since a version of their language is in common
use. Germans are aware, although this awareness is not universal, that it was only by the narrowest of votes that their language
did not become the official tongue of the new power across the
Atlantic. And what a difference it would have made to modern
history had that vote gone the other way—would there have
been a Hitler, a Second World War? Italians and Irish and Jews
of many nationalities feel a sense of ownership. Presently,
immigrants from the south of the Americas will have a case. The
Welsh—and it certainly must have seemed so to the newly
married Humphreys when they arrived in Chicago before the
turn of the century—had diminished in their influence after the
early years of the new republic. Unlike the other tens of thou-

25

sands of new immigrants to the Windy City, the Humphreys found no community speaking their language to move into, to shelter them from the economic storm that was breaking.

Chicago's pioneering years were over, and an uproarious adolescence had begun. In 1834 the Indians had been hood-winked out of their swampland on the river. For trinkets and a few bottles of whisky, Chief Sauganash abandoned a plot of land which was to be bought in 1844 for $8,000 and sold in 1852 for $3 million. For merchants and manufacturers of all kinds, the path to the West and South was open to fortunes. Wheat and cattle moved through the city; coal and iron served it. The gamblers moved up the Mississippi and the Illinois and Michigan canals to accommodate such human frailty as the whorehouses left room for. In 1865 the *Chicago Tribune* suggested that "the practice of shooting people upon the most trifling provocation is becoming all too prevalent in this city." By 1890, as more and more refugees arrived from an impoverished Europe, the English-language newspapers were suffering from German, Polish, and Swedish competitors.

Chicago was the city of the new harvester and binder made by McCormick, one of her industrial moguls. As Professor Gwyn A. Williams writes in *The Welsh in Their History:*

> The Americans invented the harvester in 1872 and the binder in 1880; they completed their vital transport network (with sub-stantial help from British money). In 1887 on the wheat farms of the U.S. northwest with wages at $25 a month, wheat could be produced for 40 cents a bushel; in the Rhineland, with wages at 6 dollars a month, wheat cost 80 cents a bushel. The Americans could produce Indian corn in the Mississippi Valley, transport it to Italy and sell it there lower than that of Lombard and Venetian corn, where laborers were paid a third of U.S. wages. In 1885, 77,000 Italian farm laborers emigrated to the U.S.A. During the 1880s over one and a quarter million people left rural Germany and over half a million quit Scandinavia; Den-mark had to rebuild itself.

What an irony, for the immigrants—driven from home by the consequences of the McCormick reaper and binder—to arrive to discover workers shot down at the gates of the very factory that had, so distantly, contributed to their poverty. Even when the Humphreys arrived in 1892, six years after the Haymarket Bomb, Chicago was dominated by that explosion's consequences. The McCormick workers had been killed because they were striking for an eight-hour day and higher wages—or rather out of a fear that wages would be lowered because of the great numbers of new immigrants coming on to the labor market. The language of their protests was mostly German. The *Arbeiter Zeitung* was the main socialist paper; the English-language newspapers called it anarchist. The press then, as later, was far more ferocious in its attacks on workers than on the supposedly corrupt Chicago political leaders.

The *Arbeiter Zeitung* had called a protest meeting in the Haymarket. The mayor was not troubled, nor was the governor of Illinois. One police lieutenant took a different view. There was a fight. Someone threw a bomb and created a tradition. The socialists or anarchists believed it came from the hand of an *agent provocateur*. The law hanged four. All—Parsons, Spies, Fischer, and Engle—made strong speeches, but in the opinion of union leaders Parsons did not help the cause of those who remained by arguing for the virtues of dynamite. What kept the memory of the Haymarket affair warm was the fashion in which the English-language press used it when the next big strike came in 1894; and the question of whether the new Governor Altgeld would pardon those convicted but not executed. The compassionate near-socialist governor did and so finished his political career.

Before the Pullman strike in 1894, which was to be so instructive to the Humphreys—as to all the other new immigrants in Chicago—they were to gather that they really had come to a theatrically rich city. Without parades and festivals, Chicago was awesome enough. The old frontier town had been destroyed in the Great Fire of 1871 (as with everything else, its fire had been the greatest ever known), and already its new skyscrapers were the most distinguished. Then, as now, the fine palaces built along State and Madison and the other thoroughfares delighted the eye; they strike one dumb: they may have been then, as now, difficult to live with in their majesty. Chicago's population, then one and a half million people, had been a few thousand sixty years earlier.

As well as rich, Chicago was—the Humphreys were to learn—as wild and disreputable a town as modern times had seen. They had moved into an apartment on Clark Street, just a few doors away from a garage where, in 1929, the St. Valentine's Day Massacre was to be staged, in which their son Llewelyn (named after his father's brother back in Wales) was held to be involved. Clark Street was one side of a rectangle—Wabash, Twenty-Second, and Eighteenth were the others—that held the area known as the Levee.

So when the young Humphreys took a stroll toward the lake of an evening and came to the Levee they would find, according to Emmett Dedmon in his *Fabulous Chicago*:

> Gambling houses, barrelhouse saloons, dance halls, pawn shops, tintype galleries, voodoo doctors, penny arcades, fake auctions and a few legitimate livery stables, blacksmith shops and oyster bars. Within the borders of a few blocks were located more than two hundred brothels. They ranged from low dives and panel houses, where robbers worked in collaboration with prostitutes, to elegantly furnished mansions governed by a strict code of conduct. A visitor to the Levee usually said he was "going down the line": he was lucky if he returned with his bait.

This is what Frank Sinatra means when, singing the twenties' "Chicago" in concert, he has an aside about "going down the line." This also perhaps explains where Mr. Evan Humphreys acquired the gambling habit, which was later to be subsidized daily by his prosperous younger son.

The Levee, so called by the dashing professional gamblers who had come from the South after the Civil War, was not to make its unique mark nor to impose its style on Chicago politics for more than another decade. In 1893 enthusiasm was directed at demonstrating to the world that Chicago was the American city with the mostest. Hadn't the Iron Chancellor Bismarck said that he would like to go to America if only to see that *Chicago?* How much more would he wish so, once the exhibition to celebrate Columbus's discovery of America had been staged. So elaborate were the plans that it would have to happen a year later than it should have happened: what did that matter?

And so it came to pass that almost seven hundred thousand citizens of Chicago followed Mayor Carter Harrison, President Grover Cleveland, and the Duke of Veragua, a descendant of Columbus, southward to the exhibition's White City, built (like Venice) on a beach. It was May Day and the crowds were to come from all over the United States until late October. The Infanta of Spain came; so did Archduke Ferdinand, heir to the Austro-Hungarian empire. The Queen of Italy sent laces that had not traveled out of Italy before, finery the Romans had stolen from Egyptian tombs in Caesar's time.

Most European nations had sent exhibits to the Exposition. Since Chicagoans were in permanent competition with Yankees on the East Coast for universal regard, these manifestations of sophisticated enthusiasm delighted more than the wealthy. Not, they'd have you know, that they paid much attention to what the Bostonian or New Yorker might think about anything. Indeed, the Chicago newspapers seldom reported events outside their domain. (They still don't overtax any reader's concerns abroad.) But, on the other hand, the patronizing tone of the Eastern previews of the famous event had been insufferable. For example: Chicago women did not know how to dress; at their parties they did not have people who knew even how to pour wine properly.

But my, how the snobbish New Yorkers had been shown up by events. So how sad that, on the very day the Columbian jamboree concluded, the city's popular Democrat Mayor Carter Harrison, the man who had fought off a Republican with a plan to close the Levee during the Exposition, their local hero should be murdered by an assassin with no serious complaint in his demented mind. If this canker in the rose of the year was to distress and impress the new immigrants, its malignant spread within months was to touch them more nearly.

The tough, dreadful working conditions in the stockyards and factories of Chicago at the turn of the century were to be described by novelists Theodore Dreiser and Upton Sinclair with such force, with such impassioned detail, as to create a new kind of literature. The Humphreys family from mid-Wales was to be the raw material of transforming fiction, always a less satisfying role. They worked in the stockyards, caught up in the trough of that cycle of depression and boom that then as now is governed throughout the world by the mysterious spirit of the United States' market. For the Humphreys, though, the historic conflict that involved them in Chicago in the early nineties was peculiarly poignant.

George M. Pullman, the railway baron who provoked a murderous strike, was an uncannily perverse capitalist image of the Robert Owen of their homeland. Owen was the employer who believed in the goodness of man, in the common weal. Ten miles from Chicago, George Pullman built a city in his own name for his workers, one as attractive in design as anything Owen might have wished; it was just that his purpose was different. It sounded good:

> Such advantages and surroundings make better workmen by removing them from the feeling of discontent and desire for change which so generally characterize the American workman, thus protecting the employer from the loss of money and time and money consequent upon intemperance, labor strikes and dissatisfaction which generally result from poverty and uncongenial home surroundings.

The difference between the Pullman and the Owenite dream was soon brought home to the Humphreys as to those Chicagoans who were shot down in the course of the distinction's revealing. In the Depression of 1893 and 1894, demand fell on the railway. Pullman wanted to reduce wages. In the stockyards men were laid off. Pullman's workers at once argued that they were barely, anyway, making a living wage. Now Pullman was reducing wages in his new Utopia, but he was not reducing his rents or his charges for electricity and the rest of life's necessities. His was a feudal not an Owenite Utopia. His impoverished workers went on strike.

"Within two weeks," as *A History of the American Labor Movement* has it,

> a sequence of events began that was to bring against the new united Railway Union all the resources that monopoly could throw against it—the United States government, the President of the United States, the United States Army, the Attorney General, the courts, the prisons, bullets and the press which outdid itself in describing what it called the "Debs Rebellion" [Eugene Debs was the union leader]. No matter how it is viewed it is an extraordinary chapter in American history. Because a trade union, with unusual generosity, tried to help some starving factory workers, all the forces of the established order were released to crush it and imprison its leaders.

Undoubtedly it was "an extraordinary chapter in American history," but one that was to have a far more subtle set of consequences for Chicago—and eventually for the United States—than any straightforward Marxist reading of a struggle between brutish capitalism and syndicalist socialism might suggest. Within the general railway strike, which spread throughout America, were contained uniquely Chicagoan features. The attorney general serving President Cleveland in Washington was Richard B. Olney, who had been a member of the board of a Chicago railway involved in the strike. He had been the lawyer for six other railway companies. He decided to send U.S. Army troops into Chicago even though Governor Altgeld told him not to. In spite of the protests of the Chicago superintendent of police, Attorney General Olney encouraged the swearing in of deputy marshals in the bars and brothels of the Levee; he had guns put in the hands of ex-convicts, thugs, and thieves, and encouraged them to shoot strikers. They did.

In July 1894 the Humphreys's new home city held 14,000 armed men: 6,000 troops, 5,000 railway deputy marshals, and 3,000 police. The hooligans from the Levee provoked quarrels; strikers responded. Thirty men and women were killed and, by varying accounts, one or two hundred were wounded or injured. Consequently Eugene Debs and other union leaders were arrested. Their principal crime was in organizing the strike across state lines. This was held to be an offense against anti-trust laws. Naturally this legal opinion caused surprise among those citizens who had seen flourish the trusts freely created by John D. Rockefeller, J. P. Morgan, Andrew Carnegie, and others whose agents had shot down a few strikers in their time.

The new migrant could make a judgment that perhaps in this new land there was one law for the rich and one for the poor. But he had thought that back in Wales. Here, though, it seemed to be the case that a man in Washington, wherever that was, working for the president, could send in troops and organize the kind of criminal who lived just down the street from him on Clark or Madison and give him an official gun, even though the local governor and sheriff objected. That was interesting.

Coming from Wales, where for better or worse a political sense is the sixth a man or woman is born with, the Humphreys could observe that in their new home there were voices with the eloquence of their preachers and politicians in the Welsh language. There was the voice of Clarence Darrow. He was another railway lawyer in Chicago, one nauseated at the conduct of his former colleague, Attorney General Olney. Darrow came to the defense of the union leader Eugene Debs and then began to refine a language which was to make him immortal a few years later in his peroration to a jury defending another union leader, Big Bill Haywood, against a charge of murder:

> I speak for the poor, for the weak, for the weary, for that long line of men who in darkness and despair have borne the labors of the human race. Their eyes are upon you twelve men of Idaho

tonight. If you kill Haywood your act will be applauded by many. In the railroad offices of our great cities men will applaud your names. If you decree his death, among the spiders of Wall Street will go up paeans of praise for these twelve good men and true. In every bank in the world, where men hate Haywood because he fights for the poor and against the accursed system upon which the favored live and grow rich and fat—from all these you will receive blessings and unstinted praise.

But if your verdict should be "not guilty" in this case, there are still those who will reverently bow their heads and thank those twelve men for the life and reputation you have saved. Out on our broad prairies where men toil with their hands, out on the broad ocean where men are tossed and buffeted on the waves, through our mills and factories and, down deep under the earth, thousands of men and women and children—men who labor, men who suffer, women and children weary with care and toil—these men and these women will kneel tonight and ask their God to guide your hearts.

The vigor of Darrow's advocacy won Bill Haywood's acquittal and many other victories for besieged trade unionists, so much so that it might be supposed his would be the prevailing tone among immigrants in their attitude toward the unions. There were several haunting episodes that suggested that it might be so. When Eugene Debs returned to Chicago from jail, a crowd of 100,000 people came to meet him at the railway station: "They wept, cheered, laughed, and cried." When George Pullman died, three years after he had broken the union in the 1894 strike, he was buried at night in a deep tomb, the coffin covered with concrete reinforced by steel. Out of a fortune of $18 million, he left his sons $3,000 a year since neither had shown that seriousness "requisite for the wise use of large properties and considerable sums of money."

How then does the shrewd immigrant, by nature indolent, imbued with the mordancy of Calvinism's sense of original sin, barely making ends meet in the stockyards, how then does he interpret these thunderous battles in a city about to become one of the wealthiest the world has known? His religion taught him that all flesh is grass. But there *is* that time in between. He hears quoted that noble remark of his new country's savior and his state's hero, Abraham Lincoln: "Liberty before property; the man before the dollar." Yet Chicago's question has it: "If you're so smart, why ain't you rich?"

If the Humphreys themselves were not to make sense of this rich culture, their son Llewelyn, born just before the century's end, had little difficulty. Indeed he was to resolve the conflict between capitalist and trade union in a uniquely disgraceful fashion, one that the original robber barons such as Rockefeller, Vanderbilt, Morgan, and Pullman would have found astonishing, while eloquent idealists like Debs, Haywood, Jim Hill, or Darrow would have been shocked.

He was to exploit both.

4

The Mobs before Prohibition

Chicago: first in violence, deepest in dirt, loud, lawless, unlovely, ill-smelling, irreverent, new, an overgrown gawk of a village, the "tough" among cities, a spectacle for the nation.

—Lincoln Steffens

Black Powder Bombs $100
Dynamite Bombs $500
Guaranteed Contracts $1000
—Chicago mob tariff, 1920

The Democratic party (in Chicago) is built upon bribery, intimidation, bulldozing of every kind, knifing, shooting and the whole swimming in whiskey.
—William T. Stead, 1893

Llewelyn Morris Humphreys was born in April 1899, the second son of parents who were never even to try to become American citizens. Until their son became notorious, this hedging of bets, this passion for their homeland, was of little interest to anyone since they were people of no account. Subsequently it was to be thought an odd trait, this lack of any desire to be members of the greatest nation on earth.

Ann and Evan Humphreys had from the beginning little

control over their bright and belligerent son. Coming from a society where every parent's ambition was to see a child do well in the new order of schools, thrust into a chaos where strong if ineffective efforts were being made to create a new America through education, they threw up their hands. Llewelyn left school at the age of seven and never returned. Later, when Presidents Truman and Eisenhower were to remark on what a cultivated and educated man he seemed, especially for a mobster chief, Llewelyn would claim that he had been to high school, even to college. It was not true.

Seven is an impressionable age. For many of us a taste for music or games is formed then and endures a lifetime. Freudians would propose that the betrayal of Christ was created in the childhood of Judas. (Non-Freudians should respond that Judas did not *have* to do it.) At seven Humphreys was selling newspapers in the Loop in Chicago. His motive might well have been to earn some money to help his impoverished parents, since there is evidence enough that he was generous toward them throughout their life. The consequence of this innocent childish wish was a startling, physical awareness of life in the asphalt jungle, as American cities came to be known: those twenty thousand streets under the everlasting Chicago sky.

To offer newspapers for sale in Chicago in 1907 was not a simple matter of the papers being dropped at a street corner and placing them on your stand, or running with them under your arm and offering them to a customer. If you were a *Tribune* boy you had to watch out for the *Herald-Examiner* boy and watch out for yourself. As your batch of papers arrived, a few thugs might arrive simultaneously and try to snatch them from you. Therefore you needed a few heavies in your support. It might be that your copies would never arrive. Even between the presses on the Chicago River and your corner in the Loop, the truck might have been hijacked and set alight, the middlemen thumped unconscious. Journalism was not exempt from the operation of the Chicago interpretation of market forces. The principal exponent of thuggery in newspaper-selling when Humphreys was seven years old was the sixteen-year-old Dion O'Banion, who would, when Prohibition came, be the leader of the Irish gang against the Italians and their new boss Al Capone.

In the years between starting to sell newspapers in Chicago and being sent to jail at the age of eighteen for theft, Llewelyn Humphreys was taken up by a Chicago judge, Jack Murray. His life was to be transformed. Usually in history, when accounts are written of a meeting that leads to a higher plateau, to a revelation, or even to a sweet trip down a primrose path, we comprehend the character of the transformation. When Faust meets Mephistopheles we know what is in store; similarly what happens to Keats on first opening Chapman's *Homer;* Bunyan was clear about *Pilgrim's Progress.* Defending the Humphreys experience is more unusual. Here was the adolescent petty crook; there was Judge Murray, a junior figure in the electoral confusions of Chicago law, a bachelor, otherwise unremarkable. One consequence might have been that for Humphreys the judge offered the possibility of a law-abiding life. The thief might have seen the error of his ways. Or he might have amended his ways slightly and become a Chicago lawyer.

What seems to have happened is rare, indeed. Humphreys did learn lessons from the judge, but they were lessons that were to legalize crime, pervert justice, and hold up to American society a mirror so mocking as to upstage not merely Caliban but the Senate, even the presidency.

To honor the judge, Humphreys abandoned his Christian names, Llewelyn Morris—he was to be known ever afterward as Murray. Quite where and when the newspaper seller met the judge is unknown; Humphreys did not go into detail. The best guess is that it was in 1913, when Humphreys was thirteen. Given the democratic system whereby judges, like district attorneys and other officers of the law, are elected, the judge would have taught young Llewelyn Morris Humphreys as much about the political system as law, the two being scarcely distinguishable.

The young criminal, like most young people, is not usually interested in the politics of local government. If there is a shop to be robbed, a bank raided, a citizen to be kidnapped, a family to be intimidated or, as he grows in his trade, a rival to be shot, then a study of the balance of parties in City Hall would not normally seem to be required knowledge. In Chicago, however, in Humphreys's youth civic studies were peculiarly important. Even without the insights offered by Judge Murray, a brief reading of the newspaper headlines he offered for sale would have impressed the young Humphreys. In the mayoral election of 1915 there had been an upset: the Democrats had been defeated. More, a mayor had been elected so maverick in his loyalties and, even for the great city, so extravagant in his changes of mood and policy as quite to confuse the underworld. This mayor was Big Bill Thompson.

Until his election, certain decencies obtained. The place had been run since the turn of the century by two Democrats—John "the Bath" Coughlin and Michael "Hinky Dink" Kenna. The Bath owed his nickname to being the proprietor of the bath-houses, meeting places of political importance since, like bars, they encouraged conversation. Hinky Dink meant a little fellow, well-met. Each had come to power through the Irish connection and its consequent extension of the Irish belief that it was the duty of a family to help itself. This Irish Catholic view of politics—to be supported by the comparable Italian Catholic attitude—was also important in Boston and New York and, later, in Dublin. Protestant concepts of objective fairness or justice, the disinterested judgment between contestants, which had been aimed at by the founders of the United States, were alien to the spirit of Chicago.

The Bath and Hinky Dink gave parties of a kind so vast that by the second decade of the century the police had called a halt. They controlled the First Ward, which covered the Loop. Each was an alderman. They had made graft (or, as it was known to them, boodle) the accepted grease in the wheels of government and trade. Even in 1910 an alderman could expect to make $20,000 a year helping along a contractor or an insurance agent. The Bath and Hinky Dink had gathered around them a crowd of aldermen, whom one Chicago mayor described as a "low-browed, dull-witted, base-minded gang of plug-uglies with no outstanding characteristic beyond an unquenchable lust for money."

As the mayoral election of 1915 approached, Big Jim Colosimo, Hinky Dink, and the Bath, although powerful, were uneasy. The year before there had been bad publicity for a murder arranged in the Levee. Mayor Carter Harrison II, the first Chicago-born citizen to hold the office, had proved a disappointment. Although one of the boys, a true Democrat, he had been siding with reformers. He had helped to bring about the banning of brothels in Chicago; the Levee was to be closed. Not that the law actually made for much change. Big Jim Colosimo had one day contributed to the debate by sending hundreds of his whores in all their most spectacular finery into the restaurants of the city and suburbs, as if to suggest that such would be life after the Levee was closed. Losing that argument, he set up brothels in the suburbs. Business was not much affected by reform.

But the mayor, aiming high for probity, had also caused several friendly police officers to be sent to jail. This was a serious matter for Colosimo and indeed for the aldermen: it suggested that politicians could not be relied upon. Mayor Harrison then set up a Morals Squad under Major Funkhouser and Inspector Dannenberg, a move that disturbed Captain Michael Ryan of the Twenty-second Street Police Station whose graft, or boodle, derived from the Levee brothels. Big Jim sent out two gunmen, Chicken Harry Gullet and Duffy the Goat, to put an end to the threat. Captain Ryan brazenly circulated the picture of his new colleague, Inspector Dannenberg, among friendly hoods so that they would recognize the man they were to injure or kill. The result of these maneuvers was an attack by the Mob while Inspector Dannenberg was arresting prostitutes and panderers. Two policemen were killed. The *Chicago Tribune* blamed Hinky Dink, the Bath, and Captain Ryan. Big Jim Colosimo was arrested but never charged. Mayor Harrison, though, did fire the corrupt Captain Ryan, and even appointed an honest officer. Many brothels were closed. But the *Tribune*, Republican as ever, was not assuaged. It had joined the name of the reforming Mayor Harrison with Hinky Dink and the Bath and, by inference, Colosimo. They were all guilty men. The *Tribune* wanted a new man, a hero who would reform the city and sweep away the brothels, the intimidators, the mobsters. It proposed a local playboy, William Thompson. As winter turned to cold spring in the Windy City, Big Jim and his aldermen need not have worried.

Along with that crowd of elected jokers, Chicago's mobsters had the support of an Italian immigrant whom they had helped and who in turn was to help them. Big Jim Colosimo was to become as important in the underworld as his Irish predecessor Mike Macdonald, although there is no record that he was ever to make a remark as interesting as one ascribed to Macdonald. When told he was responsible for giving Chicago the title of "Sin City," Mike said that he was shocked: he had only committed crime, never a sin. (I suspect that many aphorisms ascribed to Chicago gangsters were written by men like Ben Hecht or Charles MacArthur, journalists of the Golden Age.) Colosimo could bring in the Italian vote for the Bath and Hinky Dink, either by blackmailing the customers of his brothels and bars or by intimidation.

Big Jim had begun his career in the Levee as a street sweeper. His ability to organize fellow workers as a Democratic force had impressed the aldermen. He took the fancy of, and then married, a brothel-owner in the Levee, Victoria de Moresco, and became wealthy. He then intruded upon a sinister activity in the district. For years a group of Italians had been imposing on their fellow immigrants, demanding money on pain of bombing or more particular forms of violence. This was the "Black Hand" gang. Colosimo, in turn, offered protection against the Black Hand. In passing he offered to hire out destitute immigrants as laborers, finding them work. He seemed a good, strong friend. He followed this success by taking over Black Hand lotteries—later, other mobsters and politicians were to take over Negro lotteries to advantage. Colosimo had better "soldiers" than the Black Hand because he was winning. And as his acquaintance with the voters grew, so did his friendship with the aldermen.

Colosimo glittered. He was Diamond Jim: a diamond horseshoe on his waistcoat matched those on his fingers and suspenders. He opened a café on Wabash Avenue, where everyone had to be seen. Enrico Caruso, John McCormack, Galli-Curci. Tetrazzini, and the man who had brought all the great singers to Chicago, Campanini, always ate at Colosimo's. Customers would sing; so would waiters. The food, by all accounts, was the best in town and so, too, the wines. If Caruso and Galli-Curci had known that their host's money was mostly made in the white-slave traffic, his treatment of young girls so revolting as to lead to a change in U.S. law, they would have stayed away. (This was the café that led to the joke in Billy Wilder's *Some Like It Hot*: "We was all at Rigolettos.")

But how could a stranger to a Chicago know what was happening when the citizens had little idea?

William Thompson's candidacy and his years in office in Chicago, beginning in 1915, are matchless in eccentricity and vulgarity. No Republican before or since ever won so many votes in the city. For a fifteen-year-old minor thief and street-battler like Murray Humphreys, having events interpreted for him by Judge Murray, the 1915 mayoral election must have offered an unforgettable lesson. Here was an incomparable display of language misused in the interests of power, of hypocrisy rampant, of buffoonery exalted, the very stuff of democratic politics.

Big Bill Thompson—at forty-eight he was a famous ex-athlete now running to seed—had been a Republican alderman in the city. His family was rich. He had spent much of his life in the West, shooting and drinking. His friends spoke kindly of him: "The worst you can say about Bill is that he is stupid." He was a fierce chauvinist, fond of attacking the King of England. If stupid, he had a cunning trait in speaking to the various nationalities that made up his constituency. Among the Irish he would attack the English. Since there was uncertainty about whether the United States would be involved in the World War, he would attack the British or the Germans depending on which part of town he was speaking in.

He would remember, mostly, that he was standing on a platform of reform. He would promise the citizens that saloons would be closed; he would assure the saloon-keepers that they could stay in business. He promised those who were shocked at the amount of gambling in the city that he would crack down on crap-shooting, horse-betting, lotteries, and more ingenious methods of removing cash from the voter; he assured the gambling lobby that all was well. "I'll clean up this city and drive out the crooks. I'll make Chicago the cleanest city in the world," his peroration would run in his big voice. It was only after he had been elected that he would enliven public meetings by having a local hospital send along a lunatic inmate to appear alongside him on the platform and torment him, making out that he was a political opponent (or so Ben Hecht reports).

Thompson becoming mayor was a rare setback for Hinky Dink and the Bath. Their suzerainty of the First Ward, that key constituency in Chicago, Cook County, and United States politics, no longer gave them control of City Hall. What would happen to that intricate connection between business, police, gambling, and brothels that the Irish and Italian communities had built up so carefully over nearly half a century? They could argue, with some justice, that what they had done was not wholly bad. They had helped poor immigrants to find a place in a strange wild land, softened their hurts, and offered them a job or prospects. Indeed, the English journalist and reformer William T. Stead, if otherwise shocked by the Democratic machine at the turn of the century, had written with the Bath in mind:

> Here even in this nethermost depth was the principle of human service, there was the recognition of human obligation, set in motion, no doubt, for party reasons and from a desire to control votes rather than to save souls. But whatever might be the motive the result was unmistakable. Rough and ready though it may be, the Democratic party set in motion an agency for molding into one of the heterogenous elements of various races, nationalities and religions which are gathered together in Chicago.

Certainly Big Bill Thompson's reforming zeal ran quickly

out of breath. Within three months it had become clear to Big Jim Colosimo that his business could resume. Further, in a development that astonished the Democrats, the Republicans, with the approval of their new mayor, established a Sportsmen's Club. The annals of sporting life contain libraries of skulduggery under many titles, from horse racing through boxing and, more recently, athletics; but this 1915 enterprise in Chicago races away from the competition. Mayor Thompson invited subscriptions to the club, the fee being variable and regular. The committee was soon to consist of Chief of Police Healey, slot-machine baron Mills, and Big Jim Colosimo. This trio was to make whatever corruption existed before in the days of Hinky Dink and the Bath seem playful, even innocent, merely the exuberance of a new society.

Big Bill Thompson's victory on a reform ticket was to have as its consequence an important reversal of roles between politician and gangster. Reform meant more power to Colosimo. As John Kobler so perceptively points out in his biography, *Al Capone*, whereas before Thompson's election Colosimo had to go to the Bath and Hinky Dink, subsequently these powerful Democrats had to go to him. They had lost power. Colosimo, by becoming an ally of the mayor, had gained.

The even tenor or, as reports have it, light baritone of Colosimo's ways was not disturbed by the troubles that beset his friends. In 1917 his fellow-sportsman, Chief of Police Healey, was arrested on multiple charges of graft and bribery. The reform movement had, even after the disappointments of Mayor Thompson, not quite given up. The chief went into the dock with a handful of colleagues and gangsters, charged with taking and offering rakeoffs from the supposedly abolished brothels. They were defended by the very lawyer who had so eloquently won the acquittal of Big Bill Haywood in 1907, Clarence Darrow. And they, too, were acquitted. A great lawyer's gift is as available to the crook as to the hero of the downtrodden, although doubtless his fee was higher for the corrupt cop.

By this time, Big Jim Colosimo, like most captains of industry, had acquired a personal assistant. In the nature of things, he was a relative, a New York murderer named Johnny Torrio, who took care of the details. Torrio worked business hours and spent his spare time enjoying music. Like his uncle Big Jim, he was often at the opera. When a murder needed to be arranged he would hire a gun, being both too grand and too careful to return to his old trade. Steadily he gathered information about the other gangs in Chicago, learning much that, soon, was to be useful about the Irish boss Dion O'Banion. Torrio was a man happy in his marriage, domesticated, but cold as death.

Such, in 1919, was the balance between Mayor Thompson and Colosimo, between Republican and Democrat, between law and disorder, when young Murray Humphreys stepped from the Bridewell prison. He was a handsome boy, above middle height and with a head of glorious dark curls, on the threshold of a career more spectacular than he could ever have dreamed. The forces of good in the United States were about to pass a law which would offer the forces of darkness the chance of mayhem and wealth beyond the imaginings of the vice kings and gambling barons. Chicago had seen nothing yet.

5

The arrival of Capone

The moving trigger finger writes . . .
—F. D. Pasley, after Omar Khayyam

Anyone, therefore, who examines the deeds and the life of this man will observe nothing or very little that can be attributed to fortune; since, as was said earlier, not with the aid of others but by rising through the ranks, which involved a thousand hardships and dangers, did he come to rule the principality which he then maintained by many brave and dangerous actions. Still it cannot be called ingenuity (*virtu*) to kill one's fellow citizens, to betray friends, to be without faith, without mercy, without religion; by these means one can acquire power but not glory.
—Niccolò Machiavelli, *The Prince*, 1532

On January 17, 1920, the Eighteenth Amendment to the American Constitution passed into law. This was the Volstead Act. No longer would it be possible to make or sell strong drink in the United States of America. Prohibition, the triumph of the temperance movement, had been a long time coming. The evils of liquor were familiar: whisky, bourbon, and beer degraded working people and deprived their children of sustenance. In 1848, as the temperance cause gathered puritan strength, Dr. Barnes

Grindrod had written a polemic—*Bacchus: An Essay on the Nature, Causes, Effects and Cure of Intemperance*—which praised the American Temperance Society for its "unparalleled exertions in the cause of morals and religion and whose efforts to exterminate the most fruitful source of human misery, the use of intoxicating liquors, will ever ensure them the grateful affections of mankind, and the regard and admiration of posterity." Eighty-two years later, had such longevity favored him, Dr. Grindrod would have been beside himself with delight. "It is here at last," the Anti-Saloon League proclaimed on the eve of Prohibition, "dry America's first birthday. At one minute past twelve tomorrow morning a new nation will be born. Tonight John Barleycorn makes his last will and testament. Now for an era of clear thinking and clean living. The Anti-Saloon League wishes every man, woman and child a Happy Dry Year."

President Woodrow Wilson had tried to prevent the Volstead Act's being passed. He had an understanding of his people. If in matters of international diplomacy he was ignorant and naive, his insight into the minds of fellow Democrats like Hinky Dink and the Bath was acute. Make illegal a taste people fancy moderately and they will fancy it immoderately. Thus the Bath, at home in the First Ward in the Loop in Chicago, cheerfully if wickedly shared the Anti-Saloon League's enthusiasm for a "new nation" being born. He had laid in—his political insight as fresh as ever—one hundred thousand bottles of bourbon. He sold them immediately at double the price he had paid. Had his commercial gifts matched his political sense, he would have held on to them for three years and sold them at ten times the price.

The Bath was not alone in his perception. The Levee may have gone the way of its flesh. The new phrase was "the Loop." Between the skyscrapers of the commercial kings in the heart of Chicago there wound an overhead railway. It looped dramatically and romantically over the heads of the poor and the criminals; alongside stores of rare wealth; past cafés where dazzling talents had fun. Its more excited inhabitants might have it that the Loop encompassed the Florence of the new Renaissance; its more prosaic, that there was a killing to be made; and the idiom was never to have more force.

Nowhere else on earth was there such a talent for the markup, whether in real estate, girls, or dice. Here was a recognition that human frailty is a stuff that, unlike youth, will endure forever. Jim Colosimo, Johnny Torrio, and Dion O'Banion slipped like greyhounds from the leash. Had they been more familiar with the history of their Roman church they might have brooded on the unusual state of affairs the Volstead Act had created for the moralist. The Manichean heresy had created difficulty for popes in medieval times. This heresy—which had its origins in fourth-century Persia—held that good and evil were forces of equal power. It is a persuasive thesis, but in modern times, the idea that evil exists embarrasses fashionable explanations of human behavior. Prohibition is an interesting case for the Manichean.

Let us suppose that many of the gangsters were evil men and not, as the phrase goes, victims of broken homes. Here they were in January 1920, witnessing the forces of "good"—the temperance men and women from the countryside and the puritan enclaves in the wicked cities—delivering into their hands a means of satisfying human weakness, or sin. To wit, booze. History offers nothing to compare: virtue's triumph rewards the worst elements in the society it is attempting to save. Certainly the prohibitionists meant well. Drink and the cynicism of the brewers who produced it were demoralizing immigrant communities: Bacchus was not always laughing. Nevertheless good helped evil although the concept of evil was already vanishing in a society where it was so important to try to believe the best of everyone. Whichever irony beguiled, Chicago was well-placed to satisfy the taste for booze.

Across Lake Michigan lay Canada. Boats could bring in the high-class stuff for the rich. In the city itself, thousands of poor people could be persuaded to form an "alky-cooking" guild, making hooch. If they didn't blow themselves up operating the stills, they might blind themselves if they drank the stuff. Many dilutions, many hair-raising or poisonous cocktails, were to be brewed in devilish kitchens. To raise a glass was to lend a new nuance to the idea of taking your life in your hands. Any economist of the Chicago school must have been encouraged to see theories of the relationship of price to supply-and-demand demonstrated so near to home.

Consider the astonishment, then, of Johnny Torrio when he discovered that Uncle Big Jim Colosimo began to lose interest in the bootleg trade within months of the bonanza's beginning. Here they had a Yukon on their doorstep, a goldmine that involved little labor beyond hiring murderers and torturers; the mayor was in their pocket; the police were squared; the new morals commissioner had been fired. And all Big Jim wanted to do was to sit making conversation in his café with his friends Caruso and Galli-Curci, and dote at home on his new young wife, a serious singer named Dale Winter.

Johnny Torrio did not care for this marriage. Just as Uncle Jim had called him in from the New York mob, so he now recruited from the same gang the young Al Capone. Between them they arranged for Colosimo to be at his café one afternoon to meet some person, unknown to this day. They had appointed a murderer, who went to the café and killed Big Jim. Colosimo was the first of the great gangsters to be murdered at his place of respectable work, setting a precedent for the deaths of O'Banion, Siegel, and Giancana. Only men they trusted could come near enough to kill them, so that each died in whatever unusual comfort the knowledge of treachery offers.

Colosimo's funeral also established a precedent. The Roman Catholic Church refused rites to the gangster on the grounds that he was a divorced man, which did not prevent the mob from rustling up a Presbyterian minister, nor the Bath from kneeling beside the coffin and reciting such of the Catholic service as he could remember. Five thousand mourners followed the coffin, senators, judges and lawyers mingling with the criminals, among them Johnny Torrio, Al Capone, and Dion O'Banion. (Some $100,000 worth of flowers had been bought from the latter's shop for the occasion.) Two brass bands played "Nearer my God to Thee" and were joined in song by as bizarre a chorus as can ever have been heard in the United States or, indeed, in the history of choral singing. Breughel or Hieronymus Bosch should have been living in that hour to capture the first flowering of a new, dynamic culture: an assembly of elected representatives of the people—tarts, opera singers, murderers, ponces, lawmakers and lawbreakers alike, in a multitude of abandoned nationalities and old faiths, united in song. The subconscious of the American dream had broken cover.

There were judges who refused to act as pallbearers. One was Judge John Lyle, a Republican alderman who resisted Hinky Dink's eloquence. In his *Capone,* John Kobler reports:

> "Jim wasn't a bad fellow, John," the Dink pleaded. "You know what he did? He fixed up an old farmhouse for broken-down prostitutes. They rested up and got back into shape and he never charged them a cent."
>
> "Well," said Judge Lyle, "now that he is dead, who's going to run his convalescent camp?"
>
> "Oh, Jim sold it. Some of the girls ran away after they got back on their feet. Jim got sore, said they didn't have any gratitude."

The *Chicago Tribune* the next day reflected that such must have been the homage paid to Caesar, except that here the dead man was overlord of the underworld: "It is a strange commentary upon our system of law and justice. How far can power derived from the life of the underworld influence institutions of law and order?"

While others bided their time, Johnny Torrio had plans. He could not assume that Colosimo's power would be his although he was feared and could walk the streets unarmed. But the Four Deuces bar (so named after the address—2222 Wabash) where he and Capone were to be found did not have the social appeal of Colosimo's café. No famous opera singer or actor or rich businessman, certainly no socialite, would go near the place although it was only a few yards from the café. This was because the Four Deuces was dark and dirty and because twelve people had been murdered there in twelve months.

Whether Johnny Torrio ever sat down one day and formulated a plan, as Murray Humphreys later was to do in less violent circumstances, no one knows. He was confronting a chaos of crime and corruption of a kind seldom seen before in any nation or city, certainly not for many centuries. Chicago had a score of gangs, their leaders and foot soldiers now forgotten. Each district possessed its hoods, its bombers, its torpedoes. If the Unione Siciliane with its Mafia mode was the most celebrated and profitable, it was only one among many. There was the Polish gang run by Joe Saltis in the stockyards. The fearsome Genna brothers ran the North Side. Roger Tuohy, who was later to play so important a part in Murray Humphreys's life, was powerful on the west of the city. Tuohy's friend, the Jewish crook Hymie Weiss, played a freelance, floating role at this time. Along the waterfront the Irish hoods Dion O'Banion and Bugs Moran held sway. But Torrio and Capone occupied the largest territory to the south. Even while Big Jim was alive, Torrio had begun his policy of extending business beyond the heart of the city and Cook County, bribing his way to the creation of gambling dens and brothels in suburbs like Burnham and Cicero.

The gangs were never short of recruits. Children would have their own small groups, usually racial in form. There were hundreds of thousands of poor families in a society in which the emblems of success and manifest wealth were all around, one in which material success seemed the only ambition. Two-thirds of the population were either immigrants or the children of immigrants. When it became clear, after three years of Prohibition, that a gangster could enjoy riches without even being especially senior in the mob, an extra incentive was offered the young to join.

Out on the Gold Coast, as the grand houses overlooking Lake Michigan were known, there might be, as the Illinois Crime Survey of 1921 observed, "idealists and reformers"; in the slums, the Cadillac came as a reward for hijacking, murder, or a kidnap. The number of recruits increased rather than diminished when the serious shooting began.

Johnny Torrio had tried to avoid mass murder. He had nego-
tiated deals with the various barons, agreeing on territories in
the manner of Lloyd George, Woodrow Wilson, and Clemen-
ceau at the Treaty of Versailles. Alliances would shift, certainly,
but for three years violence between mobs was little more than in
the decades before Prohibition. After all, some four hundred
Italians were murdered in Chicago between 1895 and 1925,
victims of the Black Hand, citizens with no connection to bootlegging but killed as a result of extortion and blackmail. The
murder standard was unique in Chicago even before the Volstead Act. What helped to spoil any Torrio plan for peace was
his development of the liquor trade in such an unexpected style
as to transform the profits available and, by so doing, set alight a
forest of jealousy.

Torrio bought breweries. It was, of course, illegal to brew
beer, but if those who are duty-bound to enforce a law are
inhibited either by being bribed themselves or by knowing their
political bosses would not support a prosecution, a law has little
or no standing. Thus it was with Torrio's breweries, all five of
them. If he was taken to court, the fine would be small, and
business would resume. He became rich beyond the avarice of
any earlier princes of the underworld. His power over the speakeasies grew and, incidentally, his influence over the entertainers
who sang or played in the saloons. The enduring connection
between entertainment and crime in the United States was
formed.

All this Torrio could not have done without the help of
"respectable" brewers in Chicago who advised him and helped
him to arrange the buying of their breweries. These illegal but
open alliances were known to many Chicagoans and helped to
create the relaxed, often whimsically approving, attitude of the
city to the mobsters in the Prohibition epoch. His regular sources of supply enabled him to cut prices when it suited him, to
discomfit rival beer runners—a marketing device that did not
endear him to enemies. These were forced to depend on quality
to defeat Torrio's price policy. But quality was hard to find, and

so their rivals' response was to intimidate Torrio's customers, to hijack his trucks, and attack his private army which, by 1923, was one hundred strong.

Torrio's first lieutenant, Al Capone, became restive. Unlike Johnny Torrio, Capone was not a teetotaller. (One of the many ironies of the Prohibition period is that Torrio, Dion O'Banion, and Murray Humphreys seldom if ever drank.) Torrio's efforts to restrain Capone were not especially successful. Thus in 1922 he attracted newspaper publicity:

> Alfred Caponi [sic]. 25 years old, living at the notorious Four Deuces, a disorderly house at 2222 South Wabash Avenue, will appear in the South Clark Street court today to answer to a charge of assault with an automobile. Early this morning his automobile crashed into a Town taxicab, driven by Fred Krause, 741 Drake Avenue, at North Wabash Avenue and East Randolph Street, injuring the driver. Three men and a woman, who were with Caponi, fled before the arrival of the police. Following the accident Caponi alighted and, flourishing a revolver, displayed a special deputy sheriff's badge and threatened to shoot Krause.

The charge was not pursued after a brief court appearance by Capone. A very useful precedent was thus set.

Whether Capone was carrying his deputy sheriff's badge the following May when he shot Joe Howard in Heini Jacob's bar a few doors down Wabash from the Four Deuces is not known, but the murder may be taken as raising the temperature in the gang war. The press report the following morning carried a picture of Al Capone, with the identification:

> Tony (Scarface) Capone, also known as Al Brown, who killed Joe Howard by firing six shots into his body in the saloon of Heini Jacobs at 2300 South Wabash Avenue, in a renewal of the beer war.

The boiling point was reached on September 7, 1923, and held there to scald Greater Chicago for nearly a decade. The O'Donnell gang, an established and old-fashioned Irish group, invaded the saloon of Jacob Geis on West Fifty-First Street. Geis was happy with his supplies from Torrio and Capone and saw no reason to change to those of O'Donnell. He was beaten up. Capone persuaded Torrio that to ignore this treatment of a good customer was bad for business. Therefore the O'Donnells should be pursued. The first of their gang to be shot was Jerry O'Connor. His assassin, a Capone torpedo, was Daniel McFall, who was carrying a deputy sheriff's badge. Wits, with hindsight, were to compare this murder and that of Archduke Ferdinand in Sarajevo in 1914, and the subsequent gang war with the "Battle of the Marne."

Within weeks the tactics of mayhem, soon to become familiar to the world's moviegoers in the dramatic representations of Capone's life, were on display on street corners, in public buildings, barbershops, brothels, and speakeasies, even at the opera house. Capone may have needed a license to carry a revolver— which he obtained—but his troops, soon to number seven hundred, could buy Thompson submachine guns freely since no law existed against their use. This weapon, the tommy gun, was also known as the "piano" or "typewriter." Bugs Moran, an O'Banionite, developed the technique whereby five limousines, usually Cadillacs, would form a deadly motorcade and drive at high speed past their target, firing as many as five thousand bullets in a minute. You could always tell, the saying went, when you were near the Capone headquarters in Cicero by the smell of cordite.

Within three months, seven of the O'Donnell gang were murdered by the Torrio-Capone faction, some "taken for a ride" (another new tactic), some shot at the wheel of a bootleg truck; and these were merely the successful shootings. Spike O'Donnell, one of the leaders, was shot at nine times but not once injured. Within three years there were 138 gang killings: sixteen in 1924, forty-six in 1925, seventy-six in 1926. Clearly Johnny Torrio's attempt to preserve a system of delineated territory, where each gang could cultivate its garden and supply citizens with the produce they wanted, had broken down. So much so that Torrio decided that a serious gesture was necessary. The Genna, Moran, and Weiss gangs were often being difficult, but the most difficult of all was the Dion O'Banion mob. In the public eye the Irishman had come to seem as important as the Italians, and if Torrio deplored the Irishman's growing power, Capone envied O'Banion's glamor.

Unlike Capone and Torrio, O'Banion had been born in Chicago. His father was an Irish immigrant in the 1880s, settling in Little Hell, near Death Corner on the North Side. The son became an altar boy at the Holy Name Cathedral, then a newspaper seller, and a singing waiter. Murray Humphreys would himself sell papers outside McGovern's Café, where O'Banion would sing "Mary of Argyll" to rowdy delight. By the time of Prohibition the tenor was already a rich gangster and had shot and killed twenty-five people. His florist's shop on North State Street was one of the most popular in the city, and his gifts to the poor were celebrated.

Oddly, for one of the most expert marksmen in Chicago, he was an incompetent bank robber. Once he blew out the side of a building while leaving a safe untouched. This was put down to another characteristic: his impatience and recklessness. O'Banion smiled when he shot people and much of the rest of the time, too. The Broadway playwright Charles MacArthur, then a journalist in Chicago, used to drive around the lake with O'Banion in the small hours, gossiping, and was to ascribe much of his success with women to the flowers O'Banion would give him to offer as presents. When a member of his gang was thrown by a horse as he rode in Lincoln Park, was kicked by the horse, and died, O'Banion kidnapped the horse, took it to the park, and shot it.

It was his wild mischief that was to be O'Banion's undoing. Not content with two bold pieces of hijacking that were the talk of the town—one, seizing $100,000 worth of good whisky from a train in a freight yard and driving it away in trucks; the other, driving 1,750 barrels of the hard stuff from a warehouse and leaving behind as many barrels of water, police outriders ensuring the safety of the cargo—he decided to annoy Torrio, Capone, and the Gennas. His ferocious assistant, the Pole Hymie Weiss, tried to hold him back, taking the view that he was certain to be murdered. O'Banion never would listen to advice. The Gennas were irritating him. There were six of these Sicilian brothers, senior members of the Chicago branch of the international Unione Siciliane: Angelo, Sam, Jim, Pete, Tony, and Mike. It was O'Banion's opinion that they were invading his territory when there was an agreement that they must not. He complained to Torrio, who did nothing to help. And so O'Banion ordered his men to hijack $30,000 worth of Genna's booze. More, he refused to cancel a huge gambling debt of Angelo Genna's even though Johnny Torrio asked him, as a favor, to do so.

He then turned to the matter of Torrio and Capone and invented a drama that struck him as very funny. He would sell Torrio and Capone his share in the Sieblen Brewery for half a million dollars. Torrio agreed, happy to see the back of the Irishman. As if his bootlegging exploits weren't enough, Torrio did not care to see the way in which O'Banion was able to control more votes than himself in Cook County. The handover would take place on May 19. The police arrived simultaneously. Torrio, O'Banion, and Weiss were arrested. That nothing came of the charges for a while was neither here nor there. Torrio realized that it had all been O'Banion's idea of a joke. Like the Gennas, he lost patience. O'Banion had said "to hell with them Sicilians" once too often.

The most important Sicilian in town, however, would not allow them to murder O'Banion. This eminent figure was the head of the Unione Siciliane, Mike Merlo, who was O'Banion's only Sicilian friend. Merlo, like Torrio, had been hoping to avoid an outbreak of warfare between the gangs. Torrio and the Gennas had decided in May to rub out O'Banion. On November 9, 1924, Mike Merlo died of cancer.

Nearly $100,000 worth of flowers were bought for Merlo's funeral, many of them from O'Banion's shop. His staff had worked through the night. Capone, Torrio, and the Gennas had placed expensive orders, one of the latter brothers calling at the shop himself on the day of Merlo's death. At about noon on the tenth, a dark Jewett sedan stopped across the street from the shop. Two of the three men who stepped out and into the florist's were described later as Italians, the third as a Greek or a Jew. O'Banion's assistant called Dion from the back of the shop, and he came forward with a carnation in one hand and a pair of flower shears in another. This is taken to mean he knew the men well since, with strangers, O'Banion always kept one hand free to reach for one of the three guns he carried. The men held him and fired six bullets. The man he knew was said to be a Genna, come to buy flowers for Merlo's funeral.

Open warfare began once O'Banion's funeral was over. The Gennas, Capone, and Torrio were there, walking behind O'Banion's allies Weiss and Moran. Even the crowds at Colosimo's burial were surpassed. Twenty-six trucks were needed to carry the flowers. Ten thousand people marched behind the coffin through streets crowded with thousands more. Another five thousand were waiting at Mount Carmel cemetery. Al Capone held one of his first press conferences to offer his view of the killing of his colleague:

> Deany was alright and he was getting along to begin with better than he had the right to expect. But like everyone else his head got away from his hat. Johnny Torrio had taught O'Banion all he knew and then O'Banion grabbed some of the best guys we had and decided to be the boss of the booze racket in Chicago. What a chance!

The tone of these observations persuaded everyone that it was Torrio or Capone or the Gennas who had shot down the Irishman—as he had shot so many others. O'Banion's allies decided on revenge, and their first victims would be Johnny Torrio and Al Capone.

Torrio left Chicago in fear. While he traveled to Florida and to Cuba—with Weiss's gunmen after him but unable to get a clear sighting—Capone minded a shop that was now producing a turnover of millions of dollars a year. On January 12, 1925, just over a month after O'Banion's murder, Capone's enemies missed him by seconds as he walked into a restaurant on State Street. The death squad fired tommyguns from a limousine with drawn curtains only three feet from the café entrance. The same day Capone ordered a bulletproof Cadillac. It weighed seven tons and had windows so arranged as to make firing on the move convenient. Torrio, when he returned to Chicago a few days later, was not so lucky as Capone. Weiss and Bugs Moran reached him near his home. They had been waiting there in a Cadillac, which Torrio and his bodyguards did not seem to have noticed. The gang leader was shot in the face and chest but, as his assailant leaned over him for the decisive shot, he found his automatic pistol was empty.

Torrio survived, even chose to go to jail for a year before leaving Chicago, spending some of his fortune in Paris and Naples, and returning to a quiet life in New York. There matters were as peaceful as he had wished them to be in the Windy City. In his former territory, the team of Weiss and Moran was making more and more spectacular efforts at revenge. On September 20, 1926, they led an assault on Capone's headquarters in Cicero consisting of eleven automobiles containing some fifty gunmen. The attackers took their time in playing their "ukuleles"—the fashionable new nickname for tommy guns. Thousands of bullets smashed windows and doors, almost demolishing the façade. Thirty cars standing in the road were ruined by gunfire. But Capone had fallen to the floor as soon as the shooting started. In fact, the fusillade injured only two people. Hymie Weiss did not long survive this theatrical effort to destroy his rival. Weeks later he was walking past the Holy Name Cathedral, yards from his recently departed friend Dion O'Banion's flower shop, when assassins in a window shot him down along with his three companions. One of the latter was a lawyer, another a politician.

So brazen a display of public execution was followed by an immediate if unexpected change of tactics. Whether it was the coincidence of these shootings of so many of the gang leaders that prompted his move, or whether some dark plot lay behind it, Capone decided to discover if the gangs could establish a truce, to try to recreate the spirit that had prevailed before the O'Banion murder. The principals of the mobs met at the Sherman Hotel and drew up a treaty. There was to be an amnesty; the past was forgotten. Territories were to be fixed. The remnants of the O'Banionites would be to the north, Capone to the south, with minor territories for others. And there was to be no more provoking by false gossip, no use of the press to stir trouble. The last devices were known as "ribbing," which suggests a peculiar sensitivity among semiliterate plug-uglies. With hindsight this agreement has about it a flavor of the later pact between Hitler and Stalin, two men who worked on a larger scale than their Chicago contemporaries but often with similar methods. The pact served Capone's purpose well.

Just what crimes Murray Humphreys committed in these battles is not clear. While it is said confidently that he killed enemies, had already acquired his expertise in kidnapping, had tossed a few bombs—some of the latter at trucks carrying the bootleg booze of Joe Kennedy, father of Jack, the future president—there are no details. According to Murray Humphreys's daughter, Joe Kennedy's men threw bombs at her father. (Indeed, nearly six decades later, when I held in my hand Murray Humphreys's favorite revolver, observing the three notches on the butt, I thought it reasonable to suppose that these were from hits in the twenties, since he had no need to shoot by his own hand once his authority had been established.) However, it was a general rule that in order to demonstrate good faith, loyalty, and determination if you were a "soldier" in a Mob, you had to be a torpedo and a pineapple merchant—that is, a gunman and bomber.

Neither is it clear, unless this is yet another instance of his insight, why Humphreys should have become a soldier for Capone rather than the Irish O'Banion and the Jewish Weiss. Living where he did, near the Loop, he could have chosen to follow any of a number of leaders. Why then select a predominantly Italian group with Sicilian elements? Given his subsequent career, his decision may have been governed by his knowledge of the politics of the Loop and the First Ward from his newspaper-selling days. But this is not quite persuasive, since O'Banion and the Irish also had a connection with the Bath and Hinky Dink and the other leading Democratic fixers. Whatever his motive beyond mere consanguinity, it was the Torrio-Capone mob he joined and in which, after the departure of Johnny Torrio, he was soon to rise once the Treaty of the Sherman Hotel was abrogated.

AT THIS POINT it would be proper to consider the conscience of the murderer, the psychopathology of the torpedo, the hired gun. In most civilized societies, killing fellow human beings raises moral questions. Nations have armies, and all who have served in them are trained to kill, melodramatic as the concept may seem. Quite separate from the matter of the State's authority in ordering citizens to go out and fight, there is the literature of the anguish of the murderer in a cause he believes just. Sean O'Casey's plays are moving examples. However, to raise the question with people in Chicago who have known the prominent gangsters is not fruitful of much discussion. Rather, it puzzles. If you are fighting, you are shooting. The gun becomes the extension of the fist. When (naively, no doubt) in Chicago I tried to express to Irwin Weiner, a bondsman who had frequently gone bail for Murray Humphreys, how shocked I was that a man had been shot down as he stood next to the bondsman in a hotel car park in 1983, I realized not only that his distress was less then mine might have been, but that the concept seemed odd to him.

The responsibility for the general use of arms to settle disputes in the United States is variously allocated. There is that "frontier" tradition, although the only frontiers the Chicago mobs recognized had nothing to do with open country to the west. There are, too, the Fenian and Sicilian influences. Freudians will have their view, which would extend to the general violence of the society. Wherever the blame is laid, there is little sign that the rival armies in the Prohibition battles were much troubled over their shooting each other down. Many of the enforcers and ukulele men were psychopaths: O'Banion and Machine Gun

Jack McGurn were clearly so, Capone less obviously. With Murray Humphreys the assumption is, as his friend Irwin Weiner suggested, that he had a rough time when young, had to fight, and fell into the habits of the culture. Al Capone once reflected on the moral issue. When one gangster killed another:

> Maybe he thinks that the law of self-defense, the way God looks at it, is a little broader than the lawbooks have it. Maybe it means killing a man who'd kill you if he saw you first. Maybe it means killing a man in defense of your business—the way you make money to take care of your wife and child. You can't blame me for thinking that there's worse fellows in the world than me.

6

Murder into politics

There's one thing worse than a crook and that's a crooked man in a political job. A man who pretends he's enforcing the law and is really making dough out of somebody breaking it, a self-respecting hoodlum hasn't any use for that kind of fellow—he buys them like he'd buy any other article necessary to his trade, but he hates them in his heart.

—Al Capone, December 5, 1927

O, Thou that didst care for Nineveh and didst spare it, and Thou that didst weep over Jerusalem, dost Thou still brood over these great modern cities? We pray Thee to rule over Chicago, this young and strong, good and bad city—and out of man's worst to bring Thine own.

—The Reverend John Thompson,
Chicago Methodist Temple, 1927

That Murray Humphreys had political interests was first publicly demonstrated on the night of the Illinois State elections in 1930. The date was November 4. He was thirty years old. Police, searching for Al Capone, broke into the campaign headquarters of Roland V. Libonati, who had just won his first election as a state representative. The celebrations at 901 South Halstead Street, Chicago, were rowdy. There was piano playing and

singing. Ten of the company had left their revolvers on top of
the piano for safekeeping. Humphreys's friend, Sam "Golf-
Bag" Hunt (so named because that was where he kept his guns),
had propped his bag against the piano. The roisterers (Humphreys among them) were taken in for questioning but soon
released.

Even fifty-four years later Mr. Libonati, who went on to
higher things in the United States Congress (to the dismay of an
attorney general in Washington), still spoke with awe of
Humphreys. "His brains brought him power. He was not a man
of muscle. He had very high connections."

Humphreys was already known as "Murray the Camel." The
nickname had begun as Murray the Hump, after Humphreys,
and logically developed. His closest associates would call him
Curly. Only many years later, when Capone had gone to jail and
"the Camel" was referred to in the newspapers as "Chairman of
Crime Inc." and "Public Enemy Number One," did Humphreys acquire fresh sobriquets like "the brainy hood" or "the
Einstein of the Outfit."

His introduction into politics, as one of Capone's soldiers,
had not been subtle. Little that Capone did was subtle; "Little
Caesar," as he was already known, had been miffed that his
friend, Mayor Big Bill Thompson, had decided not to run for
office once more in 1923. A Democrat had been elected, one
William Dever, promising to reform the police department.
Capone, advised by Torrio, had decided that while it was
improbable that any mayor *could* reform Chicago, it might be as
well to take over the government of Cicero—a town, more than a
suburb, of some 50,000. His methods were not those Torrio
would have recommended.

In the April 1924 elections, the nonpartisan group that had
ruled Cicero decided that they would break up into Democratic
and Republican factions. Capone made a deal with the Republican political boss, Vogel, that from the Mob headquarters at
the Hawthorne Inn a campaign would be organized which
would guarantee victory: Democrats had best look out for themselves. Vogel's only condition was that Capone not set up

brothels in Cicero. As the Illinois Crime Survey subsequently observed of the election:

> Automobiles filled with gunmen paraded the streets, slugging and kidnapping election workers. Polling places were raided with armed thugs and ballots taken at the point of the gun from the hands of voters waiting to drop them in the box. Voters and workers were kidnapped, taken to Chicago and held prisoner until the polls closed.

A Cicero judge, appealed to by frightened voters on election day, asked Chicago to send help, which came within the hour in the form of seventy special deputies.

Polling ended in a then-unprecedented street battle between the law and Capone's two hundred soldiers, many of whom had been recruited among ruffians for this flowering of the democratic process. Among the gangsters killed was Capone's brother, Frank, a prominent murderer. His funeral was held by many to have surpassed Colosimo's in its grandeur. Cicero's elected Mayor Klenha very quickly discovered the character of the political allies who had brought about his big victory.

Within weeks, even though Mayor Klenha allowed Capone to open 160 gambling places in the town, he learned of the gang leader's beating up one of his aldermen on the steps of the town hall. Protesting, the mayor was himself beaten up. The Mob was now turning over some $3 million a day from enterprises other than bootlegging. They kept the promise not to open brothels in Cicero but compensated by intimidating the authorities in nearby suburbs like Forest View and Berwyn. As Capone observed: "These are virgin territory for whorehouses." But this success in Cicero and elsewhere did not satisfy. In Chicago, Democratic Mayor Dever was still, if ineffectually, trying to clean up the police and the aldermen. The Mob wanted Big Bill Thompson back. They had all the money they needed for a campaign. Would their favorite politician be willing to stand once more in 1927? He would.

For Murray Humphreys this election was in some ways an

aberration. The Mob was on the Republican side, while his acquaintances were with the Democratic party in the Loop, where his future was, most of the time, to lie. In this mayoral election however, the criminal element was not divided: all the gangs supported Big Bill Thompson. Capone's enemies, like Moran, and the increasingly bold lesser figures such as the Aiuppas and Jack Zuta—Capone was shortly to kill most of them—also subscribed heavily to campaign funds. If Capone was to claim that he had underwritten the candidacy, Zuta boasted that he had been the first to give $250,000 to launch Big Bill on his way. Subsequently there has been confusion between this election and that for Illinois State posts that took place the following year, as to which should properly be known as the Pineapple Election—that is, the one in which many bombs or pineapples were thrown and general thuggery and mayhem prevailed.

Big Bill Thompson was involved in both. His mayoral election, however, was relatively peaceful, partly because the mobs were united on the Republican ticket. This did not prevent its being one of the more ludicrous ever held in the Windy City. Big Bill had not abandoned his ability to be all things to all men in his four years out of office. He still placed his faith in the Chicagoans' general indifference to politics and—if not on a payroll—justified contempt for their local representatives. Thus he let the gangsters know that the city would be wide open once more. The old days would return. "I'm wetter," he cried, "than the middle of the Atlantic Ocean." However, he was against crime:

> The people of Chicago demand an end to the present unprecedented and appalling reign of crime. The chief cause of this condition is not at the bottom, not with the mass of the police department, but it is at the top, with the powers seen and unseen, which rule the force . . . When I was mayor I was held responsible for crime conditions, and properly so, and I accepted that responsibility . . . I drove the crooks out of Chicago, and will do so again if I am elected Mayor.

This ringing lie was immediately followed by the more likely declaration: "When I am elected we'll not only reopen the saloons these Democrats have closed, but we'll open ten thousand new ones."

Thompson's campaign song would be sung while the candidate on the platform wrapped himself in the Stars and Stripes:

> America first and last and always!
> Our hearts are loyal, our faith is strong.
> America first and last and always!
> Our shrine and homeland, though right or wrong.
> United we stand for God and country,
> At no one's command we'll ever be.
> America's first and last and always!
> Sweet land of freedom and liberty.

Like many a politician in difficulty at home, Thompson turned to foreign affairs. His target was King George V. "If you want to keep that old American flag from bowing down before King George of England, I'm your man . . . It is up to us, the red-blooded men and women of Chicago, to stand fast against the pro-British rats who are poisoning the wells of historical truth." Of this unusual campaign, a wag remarked: "Mayor Thompson was for America First and Capone was for America's thirst."

A contemporary newspaper account of one of his meetings at the Court Theater treats his technique in dealing with opponents. (Dr. John Dill Robertson had been a colleague of his but was now standing against him with the help of the mayor's former political idol, Fred Lundin.)

> Big Bill Thompson put on his rat show yesterday at Court Theater. With two big rats from the stockyards, one named Fred, after Fred Lundin, and the other Doc, after Dr. Robertson, the former mayor kept his audience interested as he addressed his remarks to the two rodents.
>
> "This one," he said, indicating the rat named after Dr.

Robertson, "this one is Doc. I can tell him because he hadn't had a bath in twenty years until we washed him yesterday. But we did wash him and he doesn't smell like a billy goat any longer.

"Don't hang your head now Fred," he said, addressing the other rat. "Fred, let me ask you something: wasn't I the best friend you ever had? Isn't it true that I came home from Honolulu to save you from the penitentiary?"

Big Bill then related how he lived up to the cowboy code of standing by his friends and came home as a character witness in the school board graft trial.

Thompson said he had six rats to start with, but said that Fred and Doc ate up the other four, which were smaller.

On election day there was little more than the usual chicanery of Cook County polling, much the same kind of techniques as those which in 1960 were to bring about John F. Kennedy's election as president when all looked lost for him. The important task is to insure that sympathetic election officials are appointed; mysteriously, Thompson and Capone were able to do this even though, in the normal course of things, it should have been the privilege of the incumbent Democrat. Postal votes will have been acquired beforehand and falsely filled in. Vagrants will have been placed in flophouses and paid to vote the correct way (the "mattress" vote). "Repeaters" might vote as many as ten times, using a different name and address but knowing that the election officer had been fixed. If these and other dodges failed, then there were simpler techniques, like spoiling paper ballots or throwing them away. It is held that this was the election in which "vote early and vote often" was coined as electoral advice. The phrase was ascribed to Capone but subsequently was thought to have been one of Murray Humphreys's early witticisms; certainly it is more in his mode of speech than his boss's.

Big Bill Thompson won, and there began, in the words of F. D. Pasley (who was there at the time and knew many of the protagonists), "the Chicago scene of 1927 and the first four months of 1928—a period so weird that the world sat back and gaped incredulous."

The first event was innocent. Big Bill owned a speakeasy on water, the Fish Fans Club at Belmont Harbor. The night he was elected, so many people came to celebrate that the boat sank. No one was drowned. Within the next twelve months, nearly a hundred gangsters were to be shot. The Sherman Hotel Treaty was to be forgotten; in its place came the War of the Sicilian Succession.

Capone probably did not want a battle. He was at his zenith. His friend Mayor Thompson turned a blind eye to the boot-leggers' trucks, which now drove openly through the city. If the mayor's principal assistant, Homer K. Galpin, would have to leave town because of his involvement with brewers and fixing matters for them, Capone was untroubled. He was expanding his business and had set his colleague, Murray the Camel, to investigating the possibilities of doing more work in the trade unions and business community, work for which the impetuous and trigger-happy Capone was unsuited. Whether he wanted it or not, however, the Sicilian War came about and was to have far-reaching consequences both for Capone and for Mayor Thompson, since what began as insane recklessness had direct political consequences.

The detail of the dispute was not new; indeed, its conduct was conventional, given that assassination and the rat-tat-tat of automatic weapons had become as much part of Chicago as the new jazz that Armstrong, Mezzrow, Condon, and Beiderbecke were playing in the mobster clubs. The other gangs were jealous of Capone. While rich, making tens of millions of dollars per year, they knew that Capone made more. Joseph Aiello and his brothers did not care for the fact that Capone had favored Anthony Lombardo as head of the Unione Siciliane. They made common cause with the equally disaffected Bugs Moran and Jack Zuta. They decided to murder Capone and Lombardo. However, every time they hired assassins, Capone seemed to find out—and shot them. Machine Gun Jack McGurn was sus-pected, rightly, of having this sharp anticipatory sense. When they plotted to poison Capone in a restaurant, the chef betrayed them.

In the course of these maneuvers, the police were told that Joseph Aiello was hiding with friends in a house on Washington Boulevard that overlooked Lombardo's house. But all they found hidden were several machine guns, which they took to headquarters. The police were then given another address where Aiello might be. He wasn't there, either, although they did uncover much dynamite and a note from which they gathered that their man was at the Rex Hotel. And there, finally, they found him and five other hoods, who were taken back to the police headquarters building around the corner from City Hall in the heart of Chicago. There followed the Siege of the Detective Bureau.

Within minutes of the gangsters' arriving at headquarters with the detectives, a policeman looking out of the window saw a train of taxis draw up and men run to surround the building. Three mobsters entered, and one produced a gun. The detective recognized him as a Capone torpedo, later to become prominent as Louis "Little New York" Campagna. The detective bureau had been surrounded by the Capone gang. The detectives put the three men in a cell next to Aiello. It is reported that Campagna spoke to him in a Sicilian dialect, to the effect that Aiello was as good as dead. The newspapers the next day carried banner headlines, as usual, about Capone's latest dramatic gesture—GUNMEN DEFY POLICE: INVADE LAW'S STRONGHOLD.

Editorials were angry. What kind of city was this, what kind of country was this, where a racketeer could command his troops to surround the citadel of law and order, his gunmen to stroll in armed as casually as if entering a bar? Capone was never more clearly the governor of Chicago and Cook County. The theatricality of the event attracted the world's attention, even more than did an item that had been only fully covered in the press in Italy, namely that Mayor Thompson had invited Al Capone to be among the official Chicago party to meet Mussolini's friend, Commander Frencesco de Pinedo, the round-the-world flyer.

Chicagoans dismayed at this formal status granted Capone were told, vaguely, that he'd have been there in case there was an anti-fascist demonstration. Was Capone, then, chief of police as well? What other conclusion could be drawn? As ever, neither Capone's insurgents under Little New York nor Aiello were charged after the siege was over.

Capone's rivals were to enjoy the occasional success, but each provoked a fresh slaughter. If they were able to shoot Anthony Lombardo dead on the busiest corner in the United States—State and Madison—Aiello, his brothers, and Jack Zuta were to go in response. Then suddenly, without any explanation that can be assumed true, Capone decided that he would take a sabbatical. He announced, as ever, that he was tired of being traduced, that he was merely a businessman like any other providing a service to the public. His motive, his decision to buy a house in Florida among the baroque palaces that Addison Mizner had built for the rich, near those keys where the rum-runners ran, may have been due to fatigue. He was only thirty years old, but his mode of life was not healthy—the rooms full of smoke, the drinking steady, the food heavy, a day at the races not providing much exercise. And a lot of people were being shot; perhaps his luck would run out. Or had he done a deal with Mayor Thompson?

Picking one's way through the political shenanigans of Cook County in this period would tax a commentator brought up in the period of Britain's Tudors or Italy's Borgias. Capone had issued instructions to those enduring old rogues, Hinky Dink and the Bath: they had to pay him a share of their profits from the gambling pools that had been part of the Democrats' income. Colleagues who harangued Hinky Dink at his craven behavior in being bullied by Capone were told that he was lucky to have been left any share at all. Are we therefore to assume that the Democrats would, when the time came, have their revenge on Capone and friends? Certainly the Democrats began to move closer to Roger Tuohy, a hitherto inconsiderable mobster with Irish connections, and set in process a campaign that was to lead almost to the assassination of President Franklin D. Roosevelt.

At the same time, the Republicans were about to be divided, and so violently that Hinky Dink and the Bath were happy that their heads were low.

A main cause of disturbance on the political—which was to encourage the criminal—front was Mayor Big Bill's belief that he should be Republican President of the United States. He saw a chance, on learning that Calvin Coolidge would not seek reelection in 1928. If Coolidge—of whom Dorothy Parker remarked, when that president died, "How can they tell?"—could be a president, why not Big Bill? Harding had been a Republican president and he, too, had been a crook. And so Big Bill toured the United States offering his patriotic "America First" arguments. Whether he had told Capone that his cause would not be helped—after the Siege of the Detective Bureau, not to mention the War of the Sicilian Succession—by the Little Caesar's marching through Chicago as if he owned it, is not known. What is certain is that Mayor Thompson set his police on a course of a little light harassment of the mobsters. He then prepared his campaign.

While Capone was away in the early months of 1928, his Outfit was in the hands of his accountant, Jake Guzik, more and more advised by his industrial expert, Murray the Camel Humphreys. Thompson, using his mayoral office in the Chicago fashion as a potent source of patronage, established a team that, as a first step to the prize in Washington, would contest the Illinois State elections. No doubt he hoped that the primary election campaign would be untroubled. Unfortunately for him, Capone's diplomatic absence merely encouraged others to seize the hour. A minor skirmish among disaffected gambling bosses led to Capone's friends' retaliating by throwing bombs at the homes of Thompson's "America First" supporters. A police guard was needed at Thompson's house.

Chicago's voters were quick to see that the April 1928 election was different in kind from earlier ones. Certainly vote-gatherers had been shot before, but this time the overture was something special. The Senator for Illinois, the Republican Charles S. Deneen, an enemy of Mayor Thompson, was to become involved in a manner he certainly did not seek, but that was to contribute to an uproar attracting world attention and to an unprecedented number of European journalists making camp in the city.

Part of the reason for the gathering interest lay in the decision by the Federal government to send agents into Chicago to try to arrest some bootleggers. Senator Deneen was thought to support these efforts at keeping the law. However, one of the Federal agents shot a Chicago marshal, the marshal mistakenly thinking the agents were bootleggers. Chicago's chief of police wanted to arrest the FBI man who refused to leave the federal building in Chicago. Mayor Thompson brooded on whether to launch an attack on the FBI, but was somehow dissuaded. Perhaps if Capone had been in town his decision would have been different.

At which point, an ally of Senator Deneen—Diamond Joe Esposito—a man who was to his Republican faction what Hinky Dink and the Bath were to the Democrats, was murdered. This popular, if crooked, vote-gatherer's assassination was assumed to be the doing of Capone's Outfit. Mayor Thompson, in a complicated rhetorical flourish, tried to blame Senator Deneen for the killing on the grounds that he had introduced the FBI into the city. Such a gesture, the listener was led to presume, was bound to produce trouble. For a man aiming for the presidency, Big Bill Thompson was often puzzlingly given to assuming that Chicago was a sovereign state.

His arguments persuaded no one. The Outfit was now everywhere in Chicago, beating up Deneen's supporters, bombing their houses, and shooting any mobsters who might be against Thompson. The senator's colleagues, often former friends of Thompson's, were belligerent in their eloquence. Edward Litsinger called the Mayor "a befuddled big beast, lowdown hound" who had the "carcass of a rhinoceros and the brain of a baboon." Some thirty murders were connected with the election campaign. Senator George Norris of Nebraska asked President Coolidge to withdraw U.S. Marines from Nicaragua and send them to Chicago for the primary election. Mayor Thompson could be nautical: "Bourbon has increased in price from a dollar fifty to fifteen dollars a bottle, and King George V's rum-running fleet, eight hundred miles long, lies twelve miles off our coast, so every time you take a drink you say, 'Here's to the King.'" The European journalists had not wasted time in seeing the election as a rich piece of Americana.

In the last weeks of the election campaign, the churches in the city began to offer up prayers. One Sunday, worshippers in five hundred churches of all denominations—one report has it there were 100,000 voices as one—asked that "the city might be delivered of graft and corruption at the April primaries." The next day the house of Senator Deneen was bombed. However, prayers for a large registration of Republican voters were answered, even though Diamond Joe had gone to that bourne where no votes are fixed. If these manifestations of unusual public interest dismayed Mayor Thompson, he showed no outward sign. Wrapped once more in his Stars and Stripes, he would bellow out his new song for his entertained audiences:

> Scanning history's pages, we find names we love so well,
> Heroes of the ages—Of their deeds we love to tell,
> But right beside them soon there will be a name
> Of some one we all acclaim.
> Who is the one, Chicago's greatest son?
> It's Big Bill the Builder.
> Who fought night and day to build the waterway.
> It's Big Bill the Builder.
> To stem the flood, he stood in mud and fought for all he's
>   worth;
> He'll fight so we can always be the grandest land on earth.
> He's big, real and true—a man clear through and through.
> Big Bill the Builder—We're building with you.

Al Capone returned to Chicago to supervise the polling. Senator Deneen's faction, standing on an anti-crime ticket, had its own gangs, but they were outnumbered and lacked the fire-power of Little Caesar's army. Plastered with "America First" stickers, the curtained limousines with tommy guns poised, the black Cadillacs, and the chief's armored car gathered at the Hotel Metropole headquarters. Here Capone, confident since Mayor Thompson's victory in 1927, had a suite of fifty rooms. Usually it was crowded with city hall people, lawyers, judges, and policemen passing the time of day, collecting their rewards. In April 1928 his thugs gathered for instructions, to learn fresh refinements on the way in which an election should be handled. The message was plain. If they could not persuade voters to support Mayor Thompson's slate, they were to insure that they did not vote against him; and to that end they were to use their guns, and their bombs, or at least slug people.

The gun and the bomb distinguished the tactics, were added sanctions to normal conduct. Thus if a citizen was voting frequently, and an electoral officer objected, a Capone soldier would pull a gun on him. If an officer protested when a gangster brought into a booth a heap of ballot papers marked for Thompson, he would be kidnapped, Capone informed, and a replacement sent from the pool of Thompsonites the gangster had with him at the Hotel Metropole. Thugs would call at houses and, if they discovered anyone unwise enough to say they supported Senator Deneen's cause, they would either slug him or threaten to bomb the house.

From time to time, Capone's mob and Deneen's hoods would exchange fire in the streets. One candidate on the ticket, a black, was shot and killed by a passing Capone platoon. In the inquiry that followed the election—a normal event in Chicago—it was discovered that one voter had appeared in sixteen polling stations always giving the same address, that of a riding stable: "Every horse voted," as a wit had it.

The understanding was universal that Thompson's men must win in an electorate so intimidated. The astonishment proved equally universal when it became clear that, in the votes which mattered, they had lost by a margin of two to one. For once the citizens had bothered to turn out and declare that they did not want Al Capone running their city. He simply did not have enough soldiers to bomb and shoot and defraud on the necessary scale. Throughout the United States and Europe the response to the result, to the defeat of Thompson and Capone, varied from the patronizing to the ecstatic. "There is a God in Israel," declaimed the *Kansas City Star,* from a city that could have used a minor deity itself. "The objection to having Chicago elections dominated by bombs and its everyday affairs superintended by gunmen with machine guns was an important factor in the election," wrote the *San Francisco Chronicle* in an appraisal that can scarcely have taken its readers aback. The London *Daily Telegraph* believed that "a miracle had supervened." Indeed, there was a general belief that the future would be different in Chicago, now that citizens had expressed themselves.

However, there were gangsters and politicians who interpreted the result differently, Murray Humphreys among them. Capone did not propose to change his ways—as his Outfit was to show, within nine months of the election, when it carried out the most brutal and celebrated of all its murders.

7

The St. Valentine's Day Massacre

> Wherefore it is to be noted that in taking a state its conqueror should weigh all the harmful things he must do and do them all at once so as not to have to repeat them every day, and in not repeating them to be able to make men feel secure and win them over with the benefits he bestows on them. Anyone who does otherwise, either out of timidity or because of poor advice, is always obliged to keep his knife in his hand; nor can he ever count upon his subjects, who, because of their fresh and continual injuries, cannot feel secure with him. Injuries therefore should be inflicted all at the same time, for the less they are tasted, the less they offend; and benefits should be distributed a bit at a time in order that they may be savoured fully.
> —Niccolò Machiavelli, *The Prince*, 1532

Quite what process it is in the human imagination that makes one event universally memorable, while another of the same kind of far greater import remains ignored, is impossible to explain. Consider separate bursts of machine-gun fire on St. Valentine's Day, the one in 1929, the others in 1933. In the first, seven gangsters are murdered in a garage in Chicago by other gangsters, a commonplace in that city at that time. In the second, hundreds of workers are shot by the troops of the fascist Heimwehr in a battle in Vienna between the government and

75

the socialists, which the perceptive could recognize as presaging the Second World War. Few recall the tragedy of the Austrian capital; everyone knows about the St. Valentine's Day Massacre.

The Chicago murders, it is true, have been represented in many films. Billy Wilder's *Some Like It Hot* offered a comic version. Perhaps the image is enduring because it encapsulates an epoch in American life as a painting or a novel might mirror another society's distinctive days. What happened, to Hitler's delight, in Vienna on St. Valentine's Day was complicated and in a foreign language and there were no famous movies.

Although it was said years later that Murray Humphreys was involved in the organization of the massacre, often by people who gossiped in the underworld, there is no direct evidence that the police interrogated him. That may not prove anything, either. The elements in the crime that suggest that he was involved are, first, the fact that Al Capone was actually in the office of the Miami chief of police while the massacre was taking place, a coincidence that has the mark of the Camel's sense of humor. Secondly, one of the men murdered was a speakeasy owner whom Humphreys was keen to see the end of since he was a direct rival in the protection rackets, a department of crime that the Welshman had now mastered on behalf of his boss. This foe was Al Weinshank, a member of Bugs Moran's gang. Wasn't it strange, too, that the massacre took place just twenty yards from the house in which the Camel had been born? And later didn't he call the building in which the Outfit met "Schneiders," as if after the family that had overheard the shots being fired on St. Valentine's Day? That may just have been his sense of humor, too.

The object of the exercise was to kill Bugs Moran and as many of his associates as possible, to demonstrate that the Capone mob was in charge. Moran was suspected of hijacking, or buying from hijackers, Capone's supplies of a popular brand of whisky, Old Log Cabin. To test this theory, Moran's confidence was built up in a dealer, a supposed hijacker. This double agent, now trusted by Moran, told Bugs to expect a consignment at the garage in North Clark Street at 10:30 in the morning of February 14, 1929.

Two of Capone's men were watching the scene from a house across the street. Punctually, most of the members of Moran's gang arrived; the Gusenberg brothers, Frank and Pete; Adam Heyer; James Clark; Reinhardt Schwimmer, who was not actually a member but an amateur observer of low life; and Al Weinshank. Also there was a mechanic, Johnny May, who had his German shepherd dog, Highball, with him, his leash tied to a truck. Bugs Moran, Ted Newberry, and Willie Marks were late and were to offer a useful argument against any merit in being punctual for a business appointment.

It can be very cold in Chicago when the wind blows down North Clark Street: I once had my vocal cords freeze while standing and staring at a building where Moran's garage had stood. (Rumor has it that many citizens have pieces of the place as souvenirs.) On the day of the notorious gunfire, snow was falling. A police car came down the street, once known to the Indians as the Green Bay Trail. In front sat two uniformed men, behind were three civilians. This was a genuine police car, no phony mockup. It had curtains and a gong. But at a signal from the Caponeites in the window across the street, the car pulled up at the garage entrance. This was the only error Capone's men made. The signal was to mean that Bugs Moran was inside. He was not. Al Weinshank had been mistaken for him, being of much the same build and wearing a tan fedora of the kind Moran favored. Moran and Newberry, a few minutes late, saw the police car outside the garage, assumed they had been betrayed by someone, didn't worry too much and went away.

Inside the garage the two Caponeites dressed as policemen took weapons from the gang and made them stand facing the wall. The room, by all accounts, was bleak, the temperature well below freezing, lit by a single, bare 200-watt bulb. The three men who had been sitting in the back of the police car now entered, one carrying a tommy gun, the others shotguns. The firing lasted a minute, making a dreadful racket heard around the neighborhood. Then silence, except for Highball's howling.

A lodger in an apartment nearby saw the three men leave the garage with two policemen behind them pointing guns at their backs, and assumed there had been a battle with the forces of law and order. Bravely—his name was McAllister—he went into the garage. One of the seven men was still alive: Frank Gusenberg. He was asked who had shot him. "Nobody shot me," he replied. He had fourteen 45-caliber bullets in his body. When Bugs Moran was given the news, he said, "Only Capone kills like that!" When Al Capone was told in Miami, in the warm winter sun, he said, "Only Bugs Moran kills like that."

Coming so swiftly on the heels of the election with its promise of a change of city habits, the massacre assured the world and the citizens of Chicago that Capone's power remained intact. The scale, brutality, and expertise of the shooting was awesome. The crime carried another doubt into the public mind: could those men dressed as policemen have been real policemen? It was not a wild surmise, yet the cynicism was misplaced. The police tried very hard to make arrests. Machine Gun Jack was taken in as were various other hoods, but no charges could be made to stick. As it happened, all the suspects were soon to be killed by fellow gangsters in subsequent battles, a swiftness of justice that the normal processes of law would not have achieved.

For Murray Humphreys the massacre was particularly helpful since Weinshank had gone. His death emphasizes a neglected aspect of the shooting. Because it was about hijacking a load of whisky, it has reasonably been seen as the consummation of gang warfare in Chicago. Weinshank's presence offers a different perspective since he had been a member of Bugs Moran's gang for only a few weeks. His speciality was trade union and industrial affairs, as the Camel's had become. His presence in the most brutal and reckless of all the evil plots conjured up by the principal hoods graphically illustrates the horrors of the gang's presence in the working and business life of Chicago. A civic conspiracy in which torpedoes and thugs are tolerated, because they are providing people with booze wears thinner if behavior separate from the operation of the Volstead Act is considered. Under cover of the power of bootlegging, the mobs had begun to diversify well beyond their traditional exploiting of human frailty in gambling and prostitution.

"Rackets" had grown up with Chicago and took amazing forms. Technically, a bootlegger was not a "racketeer," although he might become one as the result of his illegal business. The proper racketeer was someone who might be a union organizer or the boss of a business that appeared legitimate; or he might be a thug. In 1927 the Chicago *Journal of Commerce*, writing, surely, from the heart, expanded on the word's local connotation:

> Whether he is a gunman who has imposed himself upon some union as its leader, or whether he is a business association organizer, his methods are the same; by throwing a few bricks into a few windows, an incidental and perhaps accidental murder, he succeeds in organizing a group of small business men into what he calls a protective association. He then proceeds to collect what fees and dues he likes, to impose what fines suit him, regulates prices and hours of work, and in various ways undertakes to boss the outfit to his own profit. Any merchant who doesn't come in or who comes in and doesn't stay in and continue to pay tribute, is bombed, slugged or otherwise intimidated.

As early in his career as 1922, Murray Humphreys, according to the testimony of the Chicago Commissioner Virgil W. Peterson to the U.S. Senate in 1950, had tried to move in on the milk-drivers' union. He proposed an ingenious scheme: the union should amalgamate with the janitors' union. Together they would approach the owners or tenants of tenement blocks and tell them they wouldn't have any milk delivered unless more janitors were employed or their wages were increased. This plan was to work later. Another gambit was to extort money from people living high in skyscrapers and tell them that if they didn't pay up, the elevators would keep stopping lower down. This was successful. But these were minor episodes compared with Humphreys's exploits once he had become Capone's principal in the rackets.

At the time of the St. Valentine's Day Massacre, the Illinois attorney's office calculated that there were nearly a hundred business associations or trade unions run by racketeers. Master

Photo Finishers, the Motion Picture Operators (which the
Camel was later to use for one of his most spectacular coups), the
City Hall Clerks, the Painters and Decorators, the Jewish
Chicken Killers, the Glaziers, the Musicians, the Retail Food
and Fruit Dealers were just a handful of them. The case of the
Master Cleaners and Dyers Association and the Sanitary Cleaning Shops shows that Murray Humphreys, by 1928, had become
the master of the rackets. His style was established, his technique
polished already to that mixture of charm and ruthlessness,
insouciance and brutality that was to impress gangster, politician, lawyer, and FBI alike throughout his career, and to enrage
Attorney General Robert Kennedy in the late fifties and early
sixties.

The principal dyer and cleaner in Chicago was Morris Becker.
Over forty-two years he had built his business into ten large
establishments distributed throughout the city. In 1928 he
claimed that the Master Cleaners and Dyers Association wanted
to control cleaning. They wanted to dictate prices to him. "My
places have been bombed time and time again; my employees
slugged, robbed and threatened; then without warning they
were called out on strike. Union officials told me I would have to
see Walter Crowley, manager of the Master Cleaners. Crowley
said if I paid $5,000 and joined the Association everything would
be okay." He refused to have anything to do with them.

He was next approached by more senior gangsters Rubin and
Abrams. They told Morris Becker that there was going to be a
price rise of from 40 to 50 percent for cleaning clothes. He again
refused, at which point he was told he was going to be bumped
off. Courageously he took the association to court where, once
more, Clarence Darrow defended the monopolists, or extortion-
ers, successfully. At which point Becker turned to Capone, and
Capone turned to Humphreys.

Humphreys had already appraised the situation and had
somehow acquired a laundry business. He met Becker and five
other like-minded owners. He advised them to form a new
group, which they did. Among the shareholders in the Sanitary
Cleaning Shop were Al Capone and his faithful accountant Jake

Guzik. The new organization employed Humphreys to act as an
"arbiter" in labor disputes. He was also to use his influence to
discourage the manipulation of prices, whether increases or
cuts. He was to be employed for a year at a salary of $10,000.

Immediately he settled the strike that had been plaguing
Morris Becker, and he "persuaded" the Master Cleaners and
Dyers Association to forget about raising prices. INDEPENDENT
CLEANERS BOAST GANGSTERS WILL PROTECT WHERE POLICE FAILED
ran one headline. This episode won Capone some credit.
Humphreys modestly stayed in the background, but his triumph had an important effect in the racketeering world. He
became a kind of consultant to the underworld and that half-
world in which so much of Chicago's business, especially its
public business, operated. How had he managed it?

Humphreys had moved in on Local 46 of the Laundry, Cleaning, and Dye House Workers International Union—indeed, was
to remain in control until his death in 1965. Since he was
representing Capone he could frighten anyone. At the same time
he used his position as an owner to threaten force against the
association. He was thus in a unique position to arbitrate since
he was representing both sides. Inevitably the triumph was brief.
Soon Al Weinshank appeared on the scene to fight back for the
discomfited association. Since the Camel had Capone's backing,
Weinshank went to Bugs Moran. If, on the booze front, the
relationship between Moran and Capone was held to be good, in
the legitimate laundry business the war was fierce. Humphreys
stationed his troops in a dry-cleaning plant on the South Side,
Weinshank on the North Side. It was a spectacular and nasty
contest, larger in scale—though not in kind—than others that
were the consequence of racketeering.

Humphreys' opponents were not without ingenuity. One of
their tricks was to place inflammable chemicals in a suit and
send it to a rival cleaner's. It would blow up. Humphreys relied
more on acid-throwing and bombing. In the course of the conflict, five people were murdered and many more battered. Thirty
laundries were bombed and as many damaged by acid. While
not attracting the attention of the War of the Sicilian Succession,

this racketeering touched more nearly the working life of the people of Chicago—and, in the long run, as Humphreys perfected his trade, had a more enduring effect on the country. Of course the people who had employed Murray Humphreys, men like Morris Becker whom the police could not help, who meant and hoped well, found when his year's employment was up that, suddenly, Humphreys wanted very much more money. Shall we say 30 percent of the profits? Or else? At which point, by sweet chance, his enemy Al Weinshank was shot down in the St. Valentine's Day Massacre.

Humphreys was never to look back, as the phrase goes— especially meaningful in his case, with so much to be uneasy about. His reputation was assured. Whether or not it was the laundry influence, he became at this time celebrated for the elegance of his clothes. He wore his straw hat in summer. Unlike his vulgar comrades, he smiled easily and joked—as well he might, because he suddenly saw an opportunity in the death of Weinshank that he was quick to seize. Small wonder that there is a suspicion he might have had a hand in the St. Valentine's Day Massacre.

8

A change of strategy

Murray "the Camel" Humphreys and Frank "the Enforcer" Nitti are ready to surrender. They have had enough of the blood-letting. "Too many of our friends are being killed."
—Chicago *Daily News*, December 17, 1932

And thus anyone who does not diagnose the ills when they arise in a principality is not really wise; and this skill is given to few men. And if the primary cause of the down-fall of the Roman Empire is examined, one will find it to be only when the Goths began to be hired as mercenaries; because from that beginning the strength of the Roman Empire began to be weakened, and all that strength was drained from it and was given to the Goths. I conclude, therefore, that without having one's own soldiers no principality is safe; on the contrary, it is completely subject to fortune, not having the power and loyalty to defend it in times of adversity. And it was always the opinion and belief of wise men that "nothing is so unhealthy or unstable as the reputation for power that is not based on one's own power."
—Niccolò Machiavelli, *The Prince*, 1532

Murray Humphreys's practical duties were made much easier

than they might otherwise have been for two reasons. First, Weinshank (months before he was shot down on St. Valentine's Day) and Moran had recently murdered two of the most important labor figures in the city, John Clay and Tim Murphy. Rivals had thus been removed without troubling the Camel. Clay was shot because he was honest, Murphy because he was a crook who didn't care to do a deal with Weinshank.

Murphy's death was important, since he was the boss of the building workers and in cahoots with employers and City Hall. He was expert at demolishing the buildings of the uncooperative. He liked Catholic priests to appear on public platforms with him. In 1922, fourteen buildings had been blown up with Murphy's help. Since he was also boss of the Street Sweepers' Union, following in the path of Big Jim Colosimo, he could then lend further help in cleaning up the mess.

The second reason was that the Camel was the most practiced and successful of kidnappers and so found no difficulty in moving from the relatively frivolous practice of his trade in the bootlegging field to its more serious employment in industrial affairs. Among the bootlegging gangs, to be kidnapped was a mild form of threat or, at most, a nuisance if it was to lead to a truck of booze not being picked up. The sums demanded for ransom were small, although not so minute as to be an insult to a mobster's standing. In the business and union field the practice was now brutal, now devious, and brought the Camel public attention. When in 1930 the Chicago Crime Commission, searching helplessly to bring sense to affairs, decided to name leading gangsters as Public Enemies, Al Capone became Number One and Humphreys Number Two. Who was this Humphreys? Where had he come from? The press published a picture of him wearing his straw hat. He didn't look like all the others. How could a Welshman be a gangster, a gangster a Welshman? Curiosity was not satisfied. The Camel was elusive—to journalists, to historians, to the law.

In the case of Benjamin Rosenberg, a laundry owner who resisted Humphreys's agents to the point of appearing before a grand jury and testifying against his intimidators, there was a possibility that the Camel might appear in court. Rosenberg was murdered before the case could proceed. The prosecution threw up its hands. When Dennis Zeigler of the Housing and Portable Engineers Union was kidnapped and murdered, Humphreys was arrested but immediately released when it became clear that he was far away and busy when the crime was committed.

Years later, a gangster charged for a murder elsewhere mentioned in passing, during his trial, that he had been present in a restaurant in Chicago in 1929 when he had seen the Camel shoot a man and ask the assembled company if they would mind helping him to lift the body into a back alley. Humphreys responded by observing that no one was ever killed in Chicago after 1929 without himself being bothered by inquiries. The more general view, expressed by politicians, federal agents, and mobsters, was that Humphreys by the time of the Massacre had become too grand to kill. However, it is the case that different authorities place the year his apprenticeship ended variously from 1928 to 1933. Since he was a wealthy man from 1928 onward, it does seem unlikely that, given the forces he could hire, he would need to do any dirty work for himself. Especially since he had just married a girl from Oklahoma and was settling down to domestic life, one different from the style of his Sicilian and Irish colleagues.

Humphreys's success in this period was remarkable. Some 70 percent of the rackets in Chicago came under the control of men responsible to him, producing an income of $80 million a year. That cash led to workers earning lower wages than they might have, to prices for most goods and food being higher than they might otherwise have been, to fear and trouble well above the normal anguish life in a great city imposed on anyone hoping to make a living in a small business. However, his power still depended on his being Capone's man. But Capone was running into a storm that was to destroy him.

On the face of it, Capone looked secure. He had an income of $40 million a year, and if he lost a fifth of it in gambling—he was probably the unluckiest or worst gambler ever known—had he not achieved the Chicago dream? To be rich and out of jail? He had succeeded in calling a conference of gangsters from throughout the United States to set up a cartel of the kind respectable industry always aimed at, but in this case a brotherhood of crime. Capone was not a Sicilian himself, and so could not head the Unione Siciliane or Mafia. This did not trouble him, since he enjoyed a superior power: he could murder an important mafia figure like Frank Yule. He could grant an audience to an enraptured world press. In polls throughout the nation he was high on any list of the most famous Americans. But in 1931, as he put it, people started ganging up on him.

To begin with, there was no prospect of Big Bill Thompson's winning reelection as mayor. A lowdown Democrat wardheeler, Anton Cermak, was running for the Democrats and likely to win. And there were these federal men breaking into his offices and asking about his income. They had tested the ice by charging one of his brothers for income-tax evasion and winning a conviction. The Little Caesar was to be next. Strangely—or probably not, given the moralities of the United States—a failure to pay taxes was to be Capone's downfall. The slaughter he had caused, the corruption he had heightened, the terror he had brought into Chicagoans' lives, the enduring image he had created of America, all this still could have brought him a gracious old age. But he had not paid his income tax. Even here the nonsense does not end. Capone and his friends properly pointed out that J. Pierpont Morgan, perhaps the richest man in the world, a man whose agents had caused mayhem among strikers, paid no federal income tax at all between 1929 and 1932. The proprietor of the *Chicago Tribune*, Colonel Robert McCormick, a multimillionaire, chose to value his property in Chicago at $25,000 and pay taxes of $1,500. The voices of those who thought other people apart from Little Caesar might be indicted were not much heard.

While these trials were beginning for Capone—and soon his faithful accountant Jake Guzik was to be arraigned on a similar charge—Big Bill Thompson was being replaced as a mayor by Anton Cermak. Thompson had never recovered from the rebuff of the Pineapple Primary and the crimes that followed. The Democratic machine had begun to function again under the leadership of Cermak. Once more the campaign had been conducted on the promise to clear the gangsters out of Chicago. Cermak was for honest government. He would drive Capone out of town.

And it began to look as if he meant business. In no time at all ninety Capone soldiers were killed in battles, ambushed, confronted with police in unreasonable betrayals. Was this because Capone was away? Because Guzik was occupied in fighting tax charges?

At headquarters Humphreys and his colleague, Frank "the Enforcer" Nitti, were troubled. Humphreys had a mind to give in to the difficulties; already he had been graced with City Hall's compliment that he was the "brains" of the Outfit. Nitti did not have much of a mind, especially since a city officer had recently walked into the Outfit's headquarters and shot him in the head. (Later it was to emerge that the policeman shot an unarmed Nitti in the interests of a gambling deal that the new reforming Mayor Cermak had struck. The court case saw Nitti prosecuting the policeman, who kept mum on the mayor's orders.)

Given that Humphreys was working in a state of confusion among the gangs and with little political intelligence, his course of action shows an acute intuition. Because Capone had supported the Republican Mayor Big Bill Thompson, relations with the Democratic party were bad. Capone had been unpleasant to Hinky Dink and the Bath and their friends. Humphreys knew enough of ward politics to realize that Anton Cermak could not mean that he intended to put an end to the gangs. Therefore—it is not easy to empathize with the Camel in his predicament but, given his subsequent style, not impossible to guess at it—the new mayor must mean that he intended to support a gang other than Capone's.

In this judgment Humphreys was largely correct. There is a possibility, though, that Cermak had evolved a more sophisticated plot, that he had in mind to make his City Hall the gang itself, actually to formalize crime in government. This would make even deeper the hypocrisy the mayor exhibited as he stood alongside Franklin D. Roosevelt at the latter's 1932 nomination in Chicago for the presidency, listened to the eloquent promulgator of a New Deal for America, to his assault on the "malefactors of great wealth," and lent support to his victorious campaign for the White House.

But the next time Mayor Cermak stood alongside President Roosevelt he was shot in the head, and was dead within three weeks—a melodramatic event in Florida in 1933 that exemplifies, in the complexity of its motives, the problems Humphreys had been confronted with in Chicago. He had concluded that the mayor was supporting Roger "the Terrible" Tuohy's gang, an undistinguished Cook County mob of bootleggers. There was no other explanation for the way apparently unaffiliated torpedoes were shooting Capone men. There was growing evidence that Democrats were busy among the speakeasies and particularly the gambling "wheels," taking their percentage and telling the hucksters that they could look to City Hall for protection against City Hall and Capone's men. The police, that is, would be winning their rakeoff not from Capone but from within the political structure. If Cermak's policy was perfect corruption, a corruption so pure that it requires no racketeers or crooks, where had he learned such philosophical clarity?

Anton Cermak had been a coal miner. He had come young from Bohemia (later to be part of Czechoslovakia), and was thus, like Humphreys, not a part of the Irish or Italian or Sicilian groups from which the mobsters sprang. Sensibly he allied himself with the Irish faction led by Hinky Dink so that he was thought to be one of them and became an industrious vote fixer and an opponent of Prohibition. He was not a gangster; he never killed; yet he used a gangster—Tuohy—to help him create probably the most corrupt government machine Chicago had seen, one that was to be inherited after his assassination by the Democratic Kelly-Nash partnership in City Hall, to serve as a model for the criminal political mind. Why should this be so? Why should Chicago nurture such ambitions above other cities?

The problem has been confronted more or less directly by

many thinkers. One explanation is that commerce and crime are merely two sides of a coin. When gold is worshipped, morality is irrelevant. However, there were immigrants in Chicago, millions of them, who did not nurture mobsters and racketeers: Swedes, English, Germans, Greeks, hardly a soul involved. In *The Bootleggers*, Kenneth Allsop considers the question. He writes that the Irish, Sicilians, and Jews were the principal villains. In fact, there were very few Jews in the mobs. However, Allsop's thesis is:

> The Irish, the Sicilians and the Jews had one experience in common that the other racial groups had not: European backgrounds in which self-preservation had depended upon fighting and clannish solidarity against an internal enemy—the English landowners and soldiery in Ireland, the French occupation forces in Sicily, and the anti-Semitism that ringed the Jews in almost every European city. The ancestors of the Prohibition gangsters had survived by using their muscles and their cunning. Their parents came over to America with an ingrained bitter antipathy toward the theory of justice, which, in their experience was more often than not used as a truncheon of despotism, and consequently they were not so easily dazzled and drawn by the American lodestar of middle-class managerial respectability.

If there is little reason to place the Jews in the same context as the Irish and Sicilians, there remains a common factor between the latter groups, which Allsop skirts: the Irish and the Sicilians and Italians, like Capone, were Roman Catholics. Certainly they had felt oppressed at home. Yet other people in other European states had known the heel of the landlord or the alien prince and had not become gangsters in Chicago or elsewhere in America. Most Protestants or religiously indifferent immigrants led earnest and virtuous lives. Indeed, most Catholics did. They wished to create a new, free society in which they could prosper. However, it is the case that most hoodlums were Catholic and so were most of the politicians who conspired with them.

Observers of the development of crime and its relationship with the state in America are reluctant to make much of this preponderance of one faith. If sex was a taboo subject in the nineteenth century and death in the latter part of the twentieth, to ascribe behavior to a citizen's religion smacks in both epochs of a peculiarly bilious form of prejudice, one even worse than racism. No one would suggest that a gangster was so because he was a Catholic. Why, though, should crime be so much associated with the Roman version of Christianity?

Many a Protestant would suggest—has suggested—that the nature of Catholicism presents the sinner with an easy escape in this world. The confessional exculpates. The conscience does not trouble the criminal, since he regards himself as serving a power higher than himself. His behavior is not truly his responsibility. Morality is the concern of the priest. This reading would offend the truly religious, no doubt, but it was the common understanding of the illiterate layman. Murray Humphreys was to discover in the forties, when it mattered, that it was not difficult to find priests to testify to the sterling worth of fellow hoods who were anxious to be paroled from the cooler. He probably recalled, being a Protestant himself, that it was Big Jim Colosimo's divorce rather than his murderous conduct of his brothels that made the Roman Church refuse to take the gangster to its bosom at his death. There were, too, other characteristics of Sicilian and Irish society, related to their faith, that encouraged the mobsters. After all, if their common trait was that their nations had been oppressed, why was each group quite so quick to fight among themselves in Chicago, to oppress each other?

When a community has its faith taken care of, it then looks after itself. Politics becomes a matter of looking after your own. Objective standards, the pursuit of justice—all that is put to one side. Spiritual questions have nothing to do with who has this job or that, this contract or that; the politician who doesn't line his pocket is regarded with suspicion. What can he be up to? Those familiar with Irish or Sicilian politics, long after the oppressor nation has vanished, will recognize the portrait of such a community. The loyalty to the family supervenes on a loyalty to a state or any community removed from the family. Historians have proposed that the development of British cities like Liverpool and Glasgow changed in character not exclusively because their imperial role was lost, but because Irish immigration replaced the Protestant ascendancy with a Catholic one. Similarly, the connection between Chicago and these once formidable European ports from which so many migrants sailed to America was more than a sailing of heavy-laden ships. The shadow of the gunman also lay over the Irish capital, Dublin, as it does still over Belfast and Palermo.

Finding himself, a Protestant, suddenly having to solve immediate difficulties for troubled troops of different nationalities and faiths, Humphreys is reported to have been near despair. Or was it that he wished it to be thought so? Certainly it was a desperate position to be in. The chief of police called him in and told him he was finished. The problems were not only within the gang. America itself seemed to be crumbling in a Great Depression. No city in America suffered higher unemployment than Chicago. In one month in 1932, thirty-eight of its banks went bust. The gangsters found wry comfort in seeing the bankruptcy of Chicago financiers who for so long had been paraded as the good men around the place, men like Charles T. Yerkes and Samuel Insull. Many other Chicagoans found that Insull and Yerkes were more disgraceful than Capone and friends since they had stolen even more money, been more brutal in their price-fixing, more corrupt even in their political dealings. (And had not even been amusing like, say, a fine swindler and stockwaterer in New York, Jim Fisk, who was "first in war, first in peace and first in the pockets of his countrymen," although Insull, like Fisk, did give his city an opera house.) Some idea of the collapse of Chicago is given in an account by Edmund Wilson in his *American Earthquake*:

> Those who want to keep clear of the jail-like shelters get along as they can in the streets and huddle at night under the Loop or build shacks on empty lots. On whatever waste-places they are

permitted to live, the scabby-looking barnacles appear, knocked
together from old tar paper and tin, old car bodies, old packing
boxes, with stovepipes leaning askew, amid the blackened
weeds in the snow, and the bones of old rubbish piles . . . The
inhabitants of these wretched settlements chiefly forage from
the city dumps, as do many of those whom charity will not help
or who, for one reason or another, will not go to it or for whom
the relief they get is inadequate. There is not a garbage dump in
Chicago which is not diligently haunted by the hungry. Last
summer in the hot weather when the smell was sickening and
the flies were thick there were a hundred people a day coming to
one of the dumps, falling on the heap of refuse as soon as the
truck had pulled out and digging in it with stick and hands . . . A
private incinerator at Thirty-fifth and La Salle Streets, which
disposes of the garbage from restaurants and hotels, has been
regularly visited by people, in groups of as many as twenty at a
time, who pounce on anything that looks edible before it is
thrown into the furnace.

The Outfit ate in the restaurants on La Salle, as did the
ostensibly respectable "malefactors of great wealth," in Roosevelt's phrase. The hungry scratched for their leavings. The
Outfit set up soup kitchens in the city. President Hoover, who
was thought to dislike Capone for a particular reason—the press
had rushed to the gangster rather than the president when they
were at the same Miami hotel—was under the usual Republican
pressure not to help the poor and unemployed since it might
encourage them in their idleness.

Murray Humphreys did not despair. He evolved a scheme that
was to reverberate down the years (see Chapter 12). With hindsight, one can recognize, as with all his schemes, how obvious
was the solution to his difficulties, yet no one else at the time had
his vision.

If it was the case that Mayor Cermak was in cahoots with
Roger Tuohy, then something had to be done. On the other
hand, Humphreys could not be sure of this—indeed, as I suggest
in Chapter 13, had he been sure, his conduct would have been

more drastic. What he did was to frame Tuohy on a kidnap charge, the victim being a swindler by the name of John Factor. Since it was universally known that Humphreys was the master of kidnapping, there was a feeling that Tuohy had been set up.

The second part of the plan was to murder Cermak, which was accomplished in Miami to excited dismay. Here was a reforming mayor of Chicago gunned down at the side of his friend President Roosevelt. The nation mourned. But the nation, unlike Humphreys, did not know that Cermak had promised to raise gangsterism to the level of government. Not that Humphreys's concern was for the public weal; it was more to restore a more equitable distribution of the spoils between Chicago's City Hall and Cook County and the Outfit or Syndicate he was temporarily heading. Frank the Enforcer Nitti was probably behind the assassination.

Cermak had recognized that the election of Roosevelt would lead to the repeal of the Volstead Act and the end of Prohibition. His plans were set to rule the about-to-be-respectable speakeasies along with the gambling rackets. His mentors, Hinky Dink and the Bath, had been respectfully laid to rest. Humphreys had Cermak's understanding—and equally mourned the dynamic duo—and had opened negotiations already with major operators such as Joe Kennedy. The Camel's industrial experience had taught him another lesson: there was a lot of money to be made in respectable business, especially when the power of the gun lay behind commercial decisions. "Why," as Bertolt Brecht had it, "rob a bank when you could own one?"

To kill Mayor Cermak and lock up Roger Tuohy were not, in themselves, more than stopgaps in the crisis Humphreys saw facing the Outfit. The murder of Capone's soldiers had ended, and for this the troops were grateful to Humphreys or, as he saw they saw it, Nitti. Nevertheless, Capone and Guzik were going to jail for a long time for not paying income tax. (Guzik, the accountant, was not long gone; Capone was never to return. Not even the ingenuity of Humphreys could find a way to release Little Caesar from the new prison of Alcatraz off the Californian coast. He had not yet mastered federal politics.)

The suggestion is that ever since the Pineapple Primary, Humphreys had found public displays of violence both unpleasant and counterproductive, that he had disapproved of Capone's crazy murderous exhibitions in elections. This piety strikes the historian many years later as odd, given that Humphreys originally established his preeminence in the business and trade union world by way of dreadful thuggery and intimidation with acid and guns. People who knew him say he saw no contradiction but rather took a Chicagoan view that politics was one thing, business another. This may also have been part of his Welsh inheritance.

He reestablished relations with the Democratic party and met the members of the new machine at City Hall led by the Kelly-Nash group. Mayor Kelly was advancing the Cermak policy of running the gambling and saloon business. Tom Nash, a lawyer who defended gangsters, was briefly Cook County Treasurer. Humphreys came to an arrangement with them, but gave his mind more to the manner in which the Outfit or Syndicate should move forward. He bought a large Stars and Stripes flag and placed it behind the front door of his new house on South Bennet Street. About now—1933—he also bought a first edition of the songs of the Irish poet Thomas Moore, which he liked to sing, and some valuable early Dickens.

On June 27, 1933, Humphreys was indicted for defrauding the government by not paying taxes from 1930 to 1932. The Cook County grand jury also indicted him and Capone for their kidnapping, bombings, and killings in the laundry and linen business. Since Capone was in jail anyway, Humphreys was the principal defendant. As the indictment put it: "Public Enemy No. 1, heir to Scarface Al Capone's power, the brains of the so-called Syndicate and the directing agent behind the muscle men and killers who have dominated numerous unions and so-called trade associations."

The Camel did not stay in the United States to answer these charges but took a trip south of the Border, into Mexico. He stayed in Mexico for sixteen months enjoying himself with his recently married wife, fishing, shooting, and evolving a new strategy for himself and the post-Capone epoch. In 1934 he eventually returned to face the courts and, brushing aside more serious charges, was arraigned for not paying income tax on a ransom he had received for one of his kidnapping enterprises. Since he had never been arrested or charged for the kidnapping he, like others, thought it amusing that he was expected to pay income tax on a transaction that had never officially occurred. In court he gallantly asserted that he alone was responsible for whatever it was he had not done, which led to the release of others—and increased therefore the admiration for him among the criminal classes. Here was a real "stand-up guy."

The Camel went off to Leavenworth prison. "While I'm down there, I intend to study English and maybe a little geometry." While he was there, his wife Mary wrote the prison governor a letter in a prose style so elegant that had there not been the charm of the man himself, his prompt release would not have been unexpected.

There is a view that his was a tactical withdrawal, a piece of behavior rather in the style of the Duke of Wellington, whom he admired. Indeed, contrasting his approach with Capone's might have suggested an analogy: Wellington maintained that "Napoleon was looking to fight battles, I was looking to avoid them."

Humphreys certainly had not liked being represented—in the charge against him in court—as "Public Enemy No. 1, heir to Scarface Al Capone's power." When he returned to Chicago from prison, his peers recognized his eminence, but he had succeeded in making others the object of publicity. He did not want the limelight. This may be because he had learned that those in the light are shot down. In the dark, there is a long life. Or it may simply be that he was so complicated a man that he found it more interesting, more amusing, more mischievous to sit and brood and guide and fructify the Outfit so that it reached into law-abiding society.

Luck was to attend him on his release. If his plan to move the Outfit's money into major United States' corporations was already clear, the schemes whereby he was able to bring it about were smiled upon. No one will ever know where the laundered money went. It is possible to detect, though, where the Camel, by cajolery, bribery, and intellectual daring, created new oases. Quietly he asserted the virtue of his analysis and, from time to time, would offer a bravura display for the benefit of his admirers and the increasing dismay of such authorities as were not in his pocket.

9

The Double Jeopardy triumph

When any member of organized crime became involved in any kind of trial, then it was the duty of
Humphreys to mastermind the defense, the strategy
involved in defending that particular associate of his.
—William Roemer, FBI agent, in conversation, 1983

McLane's action, at the opening of the trial, brought a
smile of understanding from Murray Humphreys, one
of the seven defendants, who, like Nitti, was one of the
chiefs of the old Capone gang. He beamed upon the
man the State had expected to crush the gangsters, put
on his coat, and departed from the courtroom before
most of the crowd comprehended the significance of
McLane's move.
—Chicago Tribune, November 30, 1940

In the scholarly debates that still continue in FBI circles about
which of all Humphreys's legal maneuvers was the most brilliant, one school of thought maintains it was his novel use of the
Fifth Amendment in court and Senate hearings. At his Oklahoma home his own fretwork carving of the sentence "I refuse to
answer on the grounds that I might incriminate myself," and its
prominent place among his mementoes, shows that he himself
was proud of establishing such a precedent in American crimi-

nology. Another school holds, however, that his general conduct of the defense (nominally, Roland Libonati was the defense
attorney) in the Bartenders' Union trial in Chicago in 1940
represents a higher achievement. After all, he himself, for the
only time in his life, was on trial on a serious charge. The State
had never been so confident of success, the celebrations were
prepared, and the newspapers alerted for, at last, the defeat of the
Outfit, the triumph of the forces of the law.

The case, placed in the perspective of the city's chronicle of
mayhem, was not especially lurid. George B. McLane, who for
twenty-eight years had been the business agent of the Bartenders'
Union in Chicago, accused a Louis Romano and the Outfit or
Syndicate of interfering in the affairs of the union, stealing its
funds, and attempting to displace him. He was joined in his
action by two other officials, his brother Michael and William
Salvatore. There were 4,400 members in his local or union
branch, paying $220,000 a year in dues. George McLane was
asking for an injunction to restrain the gangsters who would
otherwise, among other serious matters, at once walk away with
$125,000 from a fund designed as benefits for members. In
support of this claim McLane's lawyer, A. C. Lewis, produced a
thirty-two-page brief that set out the history of the union and the
part the mob had played in its affairs. On the strength of it the
State moved not only against the corrupt union leaders but also
against Frank the Enforcer Nitti and Murray Humphreys. It
might not be a murder charge against two men who had strolled
away from so many, and who had commanded so many more,
but surely now they would go to jail. The charge was "conspiracy to injure a man in his employment," one punishable by "a
one-to five-year sentence in prison as the maximum."

Chicagoans were aware of the importance of the trial. It was
rich in cultural associations. The Bartenders' Union was one
supposedly respectable inheritance of Prohibition, its members
the rank and file of the legal sale of booze. There was, though, a
general suspicion that waiters and waitresses, along with the
bartenders, were being run by thugs. Joey Aiuppa, who had
procured machine guns for Dillinger and other murderers, was

thought to be involved. (Aiuppa was later to irritate Humphreys by forgetting the few words involved in pleading the Fifth Amendment before the Senate in Washington and then finding it difficult to read them when Humphreys had had them typed.) There were souls, more optimistic than history had taught them to be, who saw in the trial a vicious circle's conclusion—who, believing that such crime as they had seen, having begun in speakeasies, would now end with the bootleggers' jailing.

McLane's attorney, A. C. Lewis, certainly took a grand view of the occasion and of his fortune to have in his sights both Capone's successor as Public Enemy Number One and the Camel's nominated inheritor, Frank Nitti. He should have known better, but Humphreys's legal gifts were not then generally known.

Attorney Lewis offered the court an account, running into tens of thousands of words, of the union's origins and the Outfit's intrusions, much of it familiar, some of its 1940 rhetoric striking: "The Chicago Syndicate was the originator of the now famous Hitler policy of disposing separately of each person who interfered with its designs."

What Attorney Lewis wished to prove was that Louis Romano, who had become president of the union, and his associates James Crowley and Tom Panton, were members of the Mob; and that they had been imposed on the union by Humphreys, Nitti, and a mysterious character named Frederick Evans. (Evans, a well-known and well-thought-of accountant, was to be murdered in the late fifties by friends of Roger Tuohy—who, it was believed, had lately been killed on the instructions of Humphreys. The slogan "don't get mad, get even," always had unusual force in the Camel's conduct, but sometimes in that of his enemies as well.)

Of Frank Nitti, Attorney Lewis observed:

> He was high in the councils of the Capone gang and was generally reputed to be the person who carried out the executions decreed by the gang and became known as Nitti the Enforcer. In the course of time Al Capone was sent to prison on

an income tax charge. His gang was so well established that it
continued to function, and continued to take on new activities.
It became known as the Syndicate and the aforesaid Frank Nitti
became the titular head thereof.

The lawyer then went on to describe, in language poignant
under the circumstances, both the aspirations of the union and
the fate that befell it:

> Labor unions are usually organized as voluntary unincorpo-
> rated associations. They are intended to be very democratic in
> the management of their affairs. Their primary purpose is to
> better working conditions and establish equitable and satisfac-
> tory wage scales for the members, and for that purpose it is their
> effort to organize completely the industry to which the particu-
> lar union might appertain. The activities of the union require
> permanent officers and the establishment and maintenance of
> permanent offices . . . In many instances to protect families of
> members of the union who die they have established a death-
> benefit fund . . . In many instances said unions have prudently
> accumulated a large sum of money.

Having established the existence of these funds, Attorney
Lewis then offered an account of how the Outfit operated, a
narrative as true for all the other unions in which Humphreys
interested himself as for the bartenders of Chicago:

> The unions have become a battlefield for gang activities. They
> have developed a technique known by the slang expression of
> "muscling in." The emissaries of the Syndicate, by threats of
> violence and death, forced the unions to pay them large sums of
> money. In many instances they forced their own agents into the
> offices of the union, took charge of their treasury and of their
> business. They packed meetings with men under their control,
> and so terrorized the general membership of the union as to
> prevent the members from attending meetings. Their reputa-

tions as criminals and murderers were such that union officials and members were afraid to resist their demands.

At which the lawyer pointed the finger, on behalf of clients McLane and Salvatore, at Humphreys and Nitti:

In the year 1934 and in the early part of 1935, the Bartenders' Union through George McLane was attempting to organize the men working in the bars and taverns in Chicago. Among them were bartenders working in taverns owned by the Syndicate, although there was no way of knowing which bars and taverns were owned by the old Capone mob. The Union had pickets. Our pickets and business agents, including George McLane, were threatened. Many were slugged. On one Saturday in the early part of March 1935, McLane received a telephone call from some person who represented himself as an emissary of the Syndicate, demanding a sum of $500. McLane refused to accede to the demand, at which the emissary called and described what would happen to him if he refused to pay. Being coerced, McLane then hired Louis Romano as a Union agent. The slugging of pickets immediately ceased. The members of the picketed bars joined the union . . . Humphreys, Evans, and Romano then moved into the office and told McLane that the war was on and he would be the first casualty. Humphreys then told McLane that he would be much safer if he took a long vacation outside the State of Illinois. McLane, knowing the reputation of Humphreys, did leave the State for three months. His authority to countersign checks was revoked, and Louis Romano took over the function. By January 1940 Romano had called a meeting of all Union agents to tell them that he was the boss and that he was going to show them what muscle meant. McLane was put out of his office. The Union was controlled by the Syndicate.

The next step for Attorney Lewis was to present this powerful case in court and win an injunction for his clients, McLane and

Salvatore. To their delight, and that of the State and the government in Washington, he won. The union structure was to be dissolved. The Syndicate stooge Romano was to be fired, there were to be honest union elections, and Humphreys and Nitti were indicted on the strength of this triumph for the forces of good. The next trial, in November, would see an end to the agents of murder and corruption. If in City Hall, or in more elevated palaces of government, there were skeptics puzzled that the elusive Humphreys had been so simply netted, who tried to detect a mystery, then they were silent. Joy was, publicly, universal. Come November, so was bewilderment.

The great strategist, the puppetmaster, always has the advantage over his opponents as Humphreys was to demonstrate in this case. He knows the objective, they do not. The writer of fiction similarly has the edge; but here the Camel was manipulating not figures of his imagination but powerful elements in Chicago society and the United States. With hindsight we can see that the State of Illinois should not have been quite so shocked by the Camel's November coup. He had shown his hand earlier in the month in a different case in a different Chicago court. But since no one could see his cards, indeed not even guess at what game he was playing, the prosecutor, judge, or police can scarcely be blamed. Trying to piece his gambit together even now is not easy, its boldness still fresh after nearly half a century.

The scene is this. In the Criminal Court in Chicago a jury is, day by day, being selected and sworn in for the major trial of Nitti and Humphreys. The public is bribing court officials to win seats for the drama. Meanwhile, in the same building but in a lesser court, an odd maneuver is being conducted in a minor, seemingly routine affair that seems to have no direct connection with the big trial—except of course that it was, in Humphreys' mind, very directly connected indeed.

George McLane, the witness who was to send Humphreys to jail, was appearing in the case in the lesser court. His attorney, Lewis, was there. The honest Mr. Lewis, persuaded that within days his client was going to appear against Humphreys and Nitti and break the Outfit, was innocently offering a new argument on behalf of McLane's trade union. Whereas previously he had argued successfully for putting the Bartenders' Union into receivership so that it could make a pristine new start, he was now saying that there was no need for this receivership. His client, McLane, was now happy that the union was healthy. The crooked Louis Romano was no longer a nuisance. And, of course, Humphreys and Nitti were soon to go to jail. No longer would the gangsters be a threat.

Attorney Lewis—and who could blame him—was taken in by all this. He was a shade bewildered when Louis Romano suddenly appeared with a lawyer wishing to join in the general parade of sweetness and light. This might have suggested that perhaps there was something odd going on; but Attorney Lewis, like any reasonable lawyer, thought that he had carried out his client's instructions. George B. McLane, the good guy, had regained control of his union, was free of the dreadful Nitti and Humphreys, and was now about to appear at the Criminal Court as the key witness to help the State send the Camel to jail.

Came the opening of the big trial, the State poised, the public agog. Attorney Lewis was met in court with the news that he was no longer representing his client, George McLane. There was no time for an explanation and, had there been one possible, it's unlikely that anyone would have had the face to utter it. The vital witness would instead be represented by a former judge, Alfar Eberhardt. This lawyer was known, by those who knew such things in Chicago, to be one of Murray Humphreys's old pals, one of those judges he would place in particular courts when the needs of the Outfit demanded sympathy.

Had there been time for close analysis, the observer would have sensed that peculiar developments lay ahead. Here was McLane with his union back in his hands, having sworn that he was no longer in fear of Humphreys, arriving for the major drama without his honest lawyer but instead with one of the Camel's stooges. The Welshman strolled into the Criminal

Court, with his lawyer Roland Libonati in tow, smiling cour-teously at the assembly, placing his vicuña coat on the back of his chair and "gracing" the judge with a nod.

State Prosecutor William B. Crawford opened his case in a courtroom as crowded as the city had seen for a while—and why not, when before them they had two of Capone's inheritors, presented together for their comeuppance? Mr. Crawford ex-plained that one of his witnesses, William Salvatore, had been missing for a few months but that he expected him to appear that day to support the evidence that his union leader, George McLane, was so vitally going to offer. Prosecutor Crawford then began the recital of the testimony that McLane had offered in another court and that he was about to repeat and so harm the Syndicate. Humphreys, Nitti, and the four acolyte hoods charged with them listened to this speech by the excited prosecu-tor with, contemporary accounts have it, "polite interest." George McLane was called. The *Chicago Tribune* reported:

> In response to a question by Crawford he stated his name and gave his age as 50 years and his residence as 2911 Lunt Avenue. It was the next question which brought the bombshell.
>
> "What is your wife's given name?"
>
> "I must refuse to answer," said McLane in a voice so low it was scarcely audible, "on the grounds that it might tend to incriminate me."
>
> Q. "You know the defendant Murray Humphreys?"
>
> A. "I must refuse to answer on the grounds that it might incriminate me."
>
> Crawford asked the same question regarding each of the other defendants. McLane chanted the same answer to each question.
>
> Q. "Why do you refuse to answer?"
>
> A. "On the advice of my attorney."
>
> Q. "Who is your attorney?"
>
> A. "Former Judge Alfar Eberhardt."

Throughout the colloquy, as the *Tribune* reported, Murray

Humphreys had been beaming at the witness. The Camel was the first to put on his coat and leave the Criminal court while prosecutors, judge, police, and public sat agape. The trial was over.

The first man publicly to respond to the drama was the bewildered Attorney Lewis:

> I am sure the hand of Nitti [note: not Humphreys] reached into the Courtroom and palsied McLane with terror. There is no other explanation for his action. It may be that he still can be induced to tell the truth to the Criminal Court jury—I don't know. I want it understood that I am not a party to McLane's present conduct. When I told Judge Dunne last week that I believed Nitti had burned his fingers in grabbing the Bartenders' Union and had let go and would never again molest the union members, I made that statement in good faith. Now I am not so sure about it. I started in this lawsuit as a crusader. I expected to get results that would benefit trade unionism and the public generally. I believe we were making headway. If McLane had gone through with the prosecution of Nitti his action would have had a great influence in cleaning up rotten union affairs in this city.

Which is precisely why Murray Humphreys could not allow McLane to go through with the prosecution. For Humphreys the McLane affair was far more significant than the commonplace exercise of muscle. On the simplest level, in a fashion unusual even in Chicago, he had demonstrated to the authorities in the city and in Washington—and, more important, to the Syndicate and his friends in New York and Los Angeles—that he possessed a strategic grasp of defense. Thus he had chosen not to intimidate McLane before the trial had opened, which was the vulgar, murderous tactic of the twenties and thirties. On the contrary, he had encouraged the holding of the trial. Therefore, when the trial collapsed as soon as it opened, but after arraignment and indictment, then those charged could never be charged again for their alleged offenses. The rule of Double Jeopardy protected them: a citizen cannot have his freedom, his innocence, placed in jeopardy twice on the same charge.

Since it is improbable that the Camel went through this charade just for the fun of it—although some of his friends believe him capable of doing so—what was his objective? One colleague does hold that he wanted to try, one day, every legal gambit he had learned from Judge Murray, just as a chess player will essay an esoteric grand master's ploy, or a pianist a Bach-arranged-by-Busoni; and it wasn't long, after all, since the judge had died, and Humphreys always felt a debt. And that same colleague in the Outfit suggests, more, that Humphreys set up the whole thing, even persuading McLane in the very beginning to employ Attorney Lewis to work up a case against Nitti, himself, and others. While that reading is improbable, certainly it is the case that the consequences of the whole affair were of benefit to the Welsh-American gangster. So many lessons were carried to so many, even if it was decades before some were discovered. The McLane Affair was Humphreys's way of showing that the propaganda of the deed did not have to be the machine gun and the pineapple as in the Capone days. The new style could be witnessed in open court.

When the authorities had recovered from the shock of McLane's dreadful defection and Humphreys's affable departure—and had grasped that he had told them, in effect, not to pursue the Outfit through other unions or businesses in Chicago since the law, not Humphreys, might again get its comeuppance—it took them some time to grasp that these men were best pursued in other cities. The Camel was ahead of them even in this analysis. Indeed, it was yet another strand in his conduct of the defense that November in 1940 to demonstrate to his colleagues that he was quite in control of a far more serious game than the one they had been tormenting the bartenders of Chicago with throughout the thirties. Along with Frank the Enforcer Nitti and two other of his co-defendants that day— Louis Little New York Campagna and Paul Ricca—Humphreys was well on the way to taking over the Hollywood movie industry. His performance in the Chicago courtroom reassured them.

The Camel's repute as a stand-up guy since he had done time at Leavenworth was solid. Now he had shown that he could take the Outfit into court and mock—and win—with style. How were they to foresee that the fun their colleague derived from living on "the dangerous edge of things" was not always going to be their fun, that within four years they would be indicted and two of them jailed over the Hollywood scandal, while Humphreys was not even questioned? The third, Frank Nitti, was to kill himself when arrested in the next remarkable case.

10

Look out, Hollywood, here I come

The Outfit, through the unions, controlled every facet of the movie industry. And it all started with my mother: she was a fan, crazy about movie stars. So she mentioned to my father, why don't we go into this business so that I can meet everybody? So he, eventually, could make or break a studio by calling people out on strike. He loved making his own films, too, editing, doing the titles and putting on the soundtracks when sound came in. On holidays it was a nuisance with mother and myself twiddling our thumbs while he set up the camera.

—Llewella Humphreys, in conversation, 1983

When Nitti, Ricca, Campagna, Pierce and the others were indicted in 1943 in the Hollywood trial, the word came down that Humphreys would be charged because everyone knew he was there. But somehow it never happened.

—Art Petaque, *Chicago Sun-Times* in conversation, 1983

Humphreys was involved in that case as much as any of the people who went to jail, but the prosecution witnesses, Bioff and Browne, wouldn't give evidence against him because of their affection and regard for Humphreys.

—William Roemer, FBI agent, in conversation, 1983

Since Humphreys alone in the courtroom had known that he would have the rest of the day free, his first celebration of his double jeopardy success was to walk down Madison to the Loop and buy ten rolls of 16-mm color film. He had in mind a surprise Christmas present for his family. Throughout the thirties he had been shooting brief black-and-white 8-mm films of his parents, wife and daughter, fellow hoods. He was now going to try to make a long color film because he planned to make many more on a journey to Hawaii, Hollywood, and San Francisco.

He made the Christmas film and he made the travel films and, more than forty years later when his daughter Llewella showed them to me, I was astonished, so much so that it is difficult to unravel the skeins of surprise. First, here was the man himself, elegant and handsome as described, looking very like his friend, the actor Fred MacMurray. Here was his voice, harder perhaps than his admirers had suggested. Here were the jokes one had heard were characteristic. In one film, the ship on which he is returning from Pearl Harbor to San Francisco passes Alcatraz island, where his friend Al Capone had been imprisoned and gone mad. Here Humphreys chooses to place on the film's soundtrack the tune, "The Gang's All Here." In the sequences describing life in the Pacific islands, Humphreys the narrator offers up an earnest didacticism, to become common decades later in television documentaries about agriculture on earth in general. We learn how coffee is made. There is a dissertation on the growing of pineapples in which, reasonably enough, a giggle is barely suppressed.

The domestic film is charming. We see Mrs. Humphreys prepare the Christmas tree, bulbs alight, the presents cornucopial. The cineaste himself is seen tucking his seven-year-old daughter into bed. She pauses, then jumps out of bed and, father watching, kneels to say her prayers. And then it is the morning of Christmas, and the young Llewella opens her scores of presents, holds before her a silk dress. The delights of the day continue to be paraded. The family arrives: Grandpa and Grandma—in Welsh, *Taid* and *Nain*—the brother and sister of the host, nieces and nephews. A black servant brings in the turkey. The portrait of this happy, even perfect American family (given that they are so evidently prosperous when the Depression is not yet over) is enhanced by a brief sequence showing the head of the household at the door wearing a long vicuña coat, kissing everyone farewell alongside a large Stars and Stripes.

Humphreys's films are made with skill, enthusiasm, and affection. And while it is the case that no one who has ever been involved with any kind of filmmaking would suppose that a moral sense is a qualification for the trade—indeed, the converse could be more likely—the time and craft offered to his hobby by the great hood do substantiate his daughter's bewilderment about him. How could she square this manifestly witty and kind man with his murderous repute in the public prints? And those jolly Italians in father's more primitive black-and-white flicks, at the swimming pool in Florida, at the racetrack, fishing off their colony—Cuba, the Outfit's playground—so familial, so domesticated. Could they be murderers, too? They could indeed, and some of them, although hard to recognize in the 8-mm home movies, were to be involved in one of the cineaste's masterpieces.

It is very unlikely that the Camel needed much encouragement from his star-struck wife to give his mind, even at a very busy period in his life, to the matter of Hollywood. Chicago citizens were peculiarly aware of the cinema. The city's chauvinist newspapers reminded them that in the early days of the movies, one fifth of all the films in the world were made in Chicago. Hadn't Wallace Beery, Lewis Stone, Tom Mix, Gloria Swanson, and Edward Arnold begun their careers there? Hadn't the moguls Carl Laemmle and Adolph Zukor opened studios on the North Side before they set out for California? One version of the cause of the migration is that the country west of Chicago was being so developed that it was hard to find territory for Westerns anymore in 1910 and, moreover, the weather was terrible. Another is that the Patent Office was harassing the filmmakers and, worse, that the Chicago theater proprietors were stealing prints and making life difficult. It was easier to hide in California. True, when President Wilson, a sympathetic Democrat, came to the White House, he revoked the Patent Trust laws in 1913 and helped the Laemmles and Zukors. But by then, the

Hollywood climate had come to seem more suitable for filming.

Given that the cinema had a particular historical appeal for Chicagoans in general, for Capone's friends and inheritors the attraction was mesmerizing. To own the nightclubs where the famous jazzmen played and celebrities sang, to command the restaurants and brothels, to shoot people in the foyer in the Opera House, to have judges and politicians and cops dancing to their tune: that was life. But then to stroll through the Loop with heavily armed bodyguards and walk into a movie theater and see yourself on the screen: who in history had enjoyed such fame? Unfortunately, none of the gangsters seems to have been articulate or reflective enough to have recorded any considered esthetic appraisal of the experience of seeing their lives depicted in movies that were to entrance the world. What would Richard III or Henry IV think of Shakespeare?

That the Mob enjoyed *Scarface, Public Enemy,* and the hundreds of major or B movies that were to represent their contribution to Chicago and American culture is clear both from their attendance at the showings and their refusal to influence films in the making, when they easily might have. There is no sign that they were angry that the notorious former Chicago reporter, Ben Hecht, had begun the Hollywood stampede into gangster films with *Scarface.* The Outfit's response to the cinematic new wave was practical at first, fitful, even incoherent. There was something, or someone, missing.

Al Capone and his immediate colleagues were preoccupied late in 1929 with the fuss about the St. Valentine's Day Massacre and did not pay much notice to Tommy Maloy when he called on them. Maloy was having some trouble in his union, the International Association of Theatrical Stage Employees (IATSE). His members were the stagehands in the making of movies but more relevant, at least to the day's business, also operated the projectors in the movie houses. The structure of IATSE was such that membership was restricted so that some operators were required to pay for a "permit" to work. These latter thought this procedure a racket, and were restive. Mr. Maloy would like them persuaded of the virtue of the system.

Two very junior members of the Outfit were loaned to

Tommy Maloy. One was Willie Bioff who, by Bob Thomas's account in *King Cohn*, his biography of the Hollywood producer Harry Cohn, "had the figure of a Greek wrestler and the morals of a panderer, which he once was." The other was George Browne, "a likeable jughead and Good-Time Charlie around the Loop," as the *Daily News* succinctly put it. Bioff and Browne did not need the sharpest of minds to recognize, once they had solved Mr. Maloy's immediate difficulty by threatening a few workers, that they had arrived in a profitable office. They decided to stay. After four years of Bioff and Browne, Tommy Maloy became convinced that if he couldn't find outside help, then he would lose his union to the Mob, a way so many seemed to be going those days.

Maloy made a decision that even in the scarcely credible annals of Chicago must rank as the most crazy. Indeed, it is hard to think of any other single piece of folly with quite such consequences—not only for poor Tommy Maloy, but for his workers, for the entertainment world in the United States thereafter, and for the repute of some of the nation's most distinguished political leaders. He had heard that Murray Humphreys was just out of Leavenworth prison. He turned to "the brainy hood" to seek salvation.

It may be that Maloy had heard the word around the Windy City: the Camel had not cared for the title awarded him of Public Enemy Number One, the talk went, not merely because of his sensitive nature, his fastidiousness, but because it was unfair. It was even said that he had chosen to go to jail to remove himself from his past and its dreadful repute. And so Maloy took his concerns to this man expert in the ways of the Syndicate—the poacher, as he thought, turned gamekeeper or, if not quite that, at least a heavy neutral. Murray Humphreys was pleased to meet him. He, too, had considered the prospects of Maloy's IATSE union. More, his wife had suggested that it would be nice to take over Hollywood, to extend the Chicago business to California perhaps. He agreed to help.

Within three months Tommy Maloy was dead. As the *Daily News* put it many years later:

In February 1935, shortly after this last desperate bid to recover control of his union by asking Humphreys to get the Capone guys off his neck, Maloy was blown out of his automobile on the Outer Drive near Soldier Field by a blast of shotguns held by "dark-complexioned" men and he, like so many who had approached the flame, was carried away to another inquest at which the assassins were identified as "person or persons unknown."

Even before Tommy Maloy's murder, though, the plan was in place. The annual meeting of the union at Louisville, Kentucky, had elected George Browne as its President, any members reluctant to support him probably persuaded by the presence in the town of gangsters from most parts of America. There was Lucky Luciano, Meyer Lansky, Benjamin "Buggsy" Siegel. Less celebrated at that time was John Rosseli, a Humphreys protege who was to benefit for a while, but to meet his Maker wrapped in concrete in the Florida Keys. How sweet, though, it must have looked to Rosseli—about to be married to film actress June Lang, to be rich, to mix with the famous, to achieve the American dream: such wonders could the Camel work for his friends.

The IATSE election over, Willie Bioff was sent briskly to California. The new union president, Browne, was drinking so much by this time that nobody, including himself, knew where he was most days. Humphreys was unhappy with the state of the union in Hollywood. There had been a strike of the craft unions in 1933 that the workers had lost badly. The bargaining position was weak: the employers were too strong. A less resolute figure would have hesitated. Mass unemployment had become endemic, it seemed, in the United States. To have a job at all was good fortune. Even if President Roosevelt had just come to power with promises of a New Deal, skepticism was abroad. The motion picture industry, too, had become a means of softening the anguish of the people. Humphreys's thesis: the troubled nation needed the dream factory, did it not? His decision, action.

Before setting Willie Bioff to work in Hollywood, Humphreys placed his own brother Ernest in the business in Chicago as a cinema operator. (The city legend is that Ernest never worked even one shift; when government agents searching for the Camel went to the cinema where Ernest was supposed to be, looking for guidance, they would never find the brother but always spot several hoods in the audience watching gangster films, all on the same quest.)

The tactics to be followed at Paramount, Fox, Warners, or whichever, were familiar: first control the union, then use that power to shake down the owners. In a little over a year the demoralized union was rebuilt and much, much more. Where in 1934 there were less than two hundred union members, by 1936 there was one union only and it had 12,000 members. Those who might have wanted to see their small craft unions revived were knocked on the head. The promise from Bioff was that if everyone joined him they would have the power to stop production Where else were Louis B. Mayer, Sam Goldwyn, and Harry Warner going to find labor to make their so-profitable films? And Willie promised them a closed shop, too. And they got it.

The ground secured, it was now time for the advance. Bioff was instructed by Humphreys to approach the studio owners. Would they care to make a handsome contribution? Or would they prefer a strike? Very expensive, strikes. By 1937 Nicholas Schenck was paying $200,000 on behalf of Loew's: after all, it would be a shame if films were made in Hollywood and no cinemas in the United States were able to show them because IATSE operators were on strike. Fox, Paramount, and Warners were paying $100,000 in order to be allowed to make the movies. Columbia was shaken down for only $25,000. By Bob Thomas's biographical account, Harry Cohn alone refused to pay.

These sums from the studio owners were small compared with those the Mob was extracting from the union, not only in Hollywood but throughout America. Once Humphreys had Browne and Bioff in place and the membership had grown so remarkably in the film studios, they imposed a 2 percent levy on all 42,000 members. This brought in some $1,500,000 in 1937-38. Most of this cash went to Chicago. And if members did not care to pay this "special assessment" contribution? In Chicago, retribution was possibly less harmful than the form it took in Hollywood: in neither case was there, this time around, simple thuggery. In Chicago the Outfit double-crossed union members in a wage dispute with the circuit owners. In Hollywood it brazenly denounced its recalcitrant union members to the studio bosses as communists or anti-American radicals, insuring dismissals and setting a precedent which was to have such serious consequences in the late forties and early fifties for so many directors and actors.

It was while the gold was flowing so freely that Humphreys called at this corner of his fiefdom with family and camera. Dressed to the nines, they stroll among exotic plants with the film star Fay Wray (celebrated for her role in *King Kong*) toward a camera operated by hand and eye unremembered. Is it, the color film suggests, not passing great, as an earlier Marlowe (not Chandler's) would have put it, to be a Syndicate king and walk in triumph through Beverly Hills?

"In those days," Llewella Humphreys told me, "the studios had no tours as they have today. Joan Crawford was a very big star, at her peak then. She always worked on a closed set so that no one could come and see her. Mother really wanted to meet her. But this set that particular day was especially closed because Joan Crawford had a scar on her face in the movie and didn't want anyone to see her. The head of the studio, anyway, took mother and me in. Joan Crawford stopped right in the middle of her scene and said, 'Get those two out of here. I will not have it on my set. It's closed.' The head of the studio went over to her and told her, 'Either they stay or you go, and you are through in pictures.' So we watched her make the movie."

That the vast audiences for Hollywood productions, whether in the United States, Europe, or the growing markets elsewhere, had no idea of this close connection between the Chicago mob and the film producers was understandable enough. The law-enforcement officers, however, were equally ignorant. Since the directors, writers, and actors certainly knew the ropes, their work, with hindsight, has more force even than it seemed to possess at the time. There were many kinds of response to the gangster films, to Edward G. Robinson, James Cagney, Paul Muni and, later, Humphrey Bogart. To foreigners, at least if my youthful response was characteristic, the films were myth. The street gangster had assumed the equally mythic cowboy role; the sheriff had become the cop or the often shifty district attorney.

With hindsight we can recognize that several filmmakers were offering sharp, sometimes savage criticisms of corruption in American life. Ben Hecht and Charles Lederer were to call on their knowledge of Chicago once more in Henry Hathaway's 1947 film, *Kiss of Death*. And wasn't there even a film in which Edward G. Robinson actually played a Chicago hood who decided to go straight and arrived at Hollywood to be an actor, only to be pursued by his former colleagues in the interests of corruption? *Farewell My Lovely*, based on the Raymond Chandler novel, directed by Edward Dymtryk in 1944, is rich in sinister social atmosphere that now may look more precisely descriptive of Hollywood in Humphreys's heyday than any stranger could have deemed possible at first viewing.

Students of the American cinema have noted how many of the most distinguished talents involved in making gangster movies in the forties—Dmytryk, Hammett, Garfield, Adrian Scott— were to be hounded by the Senate Un-American Activities Committee, and were to suffer far more than Murray Humphreys ever did when the U.S. Senate tried to trip him up.

The first step was to prosecute not the gangsters but the leader of the industry, Joseph M. Schenck, who was president of the Motion Picture Producers and Distributors of America as well as of the family company, Loew's. He went to jail for less than a year, but the trial and subsequent investigations revealed that all the major companies had been fiddling their books in the interests of concealing the amount of cash that had been paid to IATSE through Browne and Bioff. The truth was out. Curiously, the revelations and the hope that the future might be a more honest one did not win the bosses of Warner Brothers, Paramount, and Twentieth Century-Fox the universal shared delight expected. There were skeptics, Bob Thomas reports, "who wondered whether the payments were aimed merely at forestalling labor trouble in the studios and the theaters. Did the company heads pay Bioff to prevent his rank and file from seeking better contracts? And did they plan to use his union to help destroy minor studios?"

The federal government now had the evidence to indict the union leaders—but in which state, which city? Since the president, George Browne, was usually in his Chicago office, the courtroom there might have seemed the obvious place. There was Los Angeles itself. Common sense, not to mention a wariness hard-won by prosecutors, proposed otherwise if there was to be a chance of winning a conviction that might stick. A discovery had been made that settled the venue. The *Daily News* reported:

> In shaking down the great minds of the movie industry, Bioff made his great mistake. Napoleon went to Moscow, after which the dice went against him. Bioff went to New York, which gave New York jurisdiction in the case even though the bundles of currency were carried to Chicago to be cut up between the individual leaders of the mob.

The Camel might always propose; he could not always completely dispose, and for reasons little different from those that preoccupied more respectable business management in America. "Personnel" was always to be a problem. Tactics had been excellent in California, income was steady, taxation nil. No one had been shot, even, although many had been leaned on. Unfortunately, not all of Humphreys's executives shared his view that life should be lived modestly—that greed, like vulgar display, did not pay either in the short or the long run. While Humphreys was content with progress—and delighted that he and his wife were making the acquaintance of and, in some celebrated cases, establishing friendships with stars of screen, stage, and radio—Willie Bioff interpreted matters differently. Bioff was taken not so much with the film stars' glamour but rather with the size of their incomes. He decided without consulting the Camel, to hound the members of the Screen Actors' Guild.

Had the president of the guild in 1940 not been an actor of such intelligence and determination as Robert Montgomery, Bioff might have succeeded. Montgomery not only warned off Bioff; he borrowed money from the guild's funds to investigate the gangster and to try to substantiate the gossip about extortion in the industry. All information was passed to the *Daily Variety*, whose editor, Arthur Ungar, also did not care for Bioff. Steadily details appeared about how much the studio heads had paid Bioff and his dipsomaniac union president, Browne. The amount of money was so great—millions of dollars—that the government in Washington paid serious attention. How should it move?

On May 23, 1941, Bioff and Browne appeared in New York, charged with extortion, and all the heads of the studios in California came east and testified. The union leaders were sentenced to ten years and eight years in jail respectively. Harry Warner, the head of Warner Brothers, made in the course of his evidence a remark that intrigued the prosecution. He testified that in making one $25,000 shakedown during one merry Yule season, Willie Bioff told him that "the boys in Chicago" wanted a Christmas present. At which point District Attorney Correa asked his assistant Boris Kostelanetz (who was brother-in-law of the opera singer Lily Pons) to discover whom the "boys" were since it was improbable that the authorities in Chicago would bend their energies in that direction. Quite why he should have imagined that any sleuth from the rival city of New York would have any luck is not clear. Certainly nothing happened until Willie Bioff, finding the dread prison Alcatraz all he feared, chose freedom and, by informing on his friends in 1943, created a sensation and guaranteed his own murder. Twelve years later, when he was living modestly in Arizona, his car blew up, and he with it, when he turned the ignition key.

Willie Bioff had reported to District Attorney Correa in New York that all the leaders of the Chicago Outfit, Capone's heirs, were the guilty men in California. There was Frank the Enforcer Nitti; Paul Ricca; Little New York Campagna; Phil D'Andrea; Frank Maritote (a relative of the Capones); Charles "Cherry

Nose" Gioe; John Rosseli; Ralph Pierce, the Camel's personal assistant; and, for local color perhaps, Louis Kaufman, the union's business manager in Newark, New Jersey.

It was "the worst blow in the history of the mob," reported Edwin A. Lacey from New York on March 19, 1943, as the federal grand jury handed down the indictments:

> The mob has sunk its roots deep in the social structure of Chicago in the past 20 years with only sporadic harassment by the local law. This worst blow has come about because the mobsters came to New York to make a few touches and thus put themselves in the jurisdiction of simpleminded authorities who operate on the theory that it is a punishable crime to steal money and shake people down.

NITTI, CAMPAGNA, AND RICCA ACCUSED IN $2,500,000 UNION RACKETS: 27-YEAR TERMS POSSIBLE ran a headline that March day, read with general approval. If there was jealousy in Chicago that their boys were being tried in New York and even some feeling that it was none of New York's business—didn't they have their own, if lesser, hoodlums in the East?—there was formal pleasure that these Capone princes would be put away. Only among very small groups in Chicago and on the West Coast, distinguished though they might be, did the extent of the indictments cause astonishment. They understood why the arrests had been made, but where—asked the politicians, the minor hoods, the specialist journalists in trade union and bombing affairs, the entertainers, the judges—where was the man himself? The master corrupter, the fixer, Capone's first inheritor, Llewelyn Morris Humphreys, Murray the Camel? Was there a misprint? Had the press missed a name?

The propaganda from the New York District Attorney's office had been such that the public was convinced that the whole Outfit had been arraigned as a result of unprecedented brilliance and courage in detection. If that was the case—as the leading Chicago mob watchers, Art Petaque among them, saw it—then clearly Humphreys must be on the list. Hadn't he murdered

Maloy's "advisor" back in the thirties in the early days? Wasn't he one of Bioff's oldest acquaintances, often seen in Beverly Hills when his arrested colleagues were not?

Many years later it became clear that the prosecution case must have rested far more heavily on the Bioff testimony than on any intrepid conduct by New York's legal legmen. Bioff had clearly chosen not to name Humphreys along with the other conspirators; therefore an indictment would not hold up against the Camel.

That Bioff's motive was simply that this particular prince was a gentleman, was so well-regarded, was held in such affection, did not become clear until much later. Only in the late fifties did the FBI become convinced that the reason Bioff would not give evidence against Humphreys, so that the Welshman would be indicted along with his colleagues, really was that simple: the Camel was held in too high a regard, was such an unusual gentleman. Bioff did not want to be responsible for Humphreys's going to jail.

There was one arcane, if low, sense in which it might have been unfair if Humphreys had been arrested with the certainty of conviction on this particular charge. His policy was to keep sources of cash, and its distribution, as closely under control as was commensurate with the fact that the sources were felonious. He could scarcely have approved of money arriving in Chicago via New York, and certainly not by any method that permitted the authorities to know that it was passing through town.

It's unlikely that the Camel was aware of the shrewd advice given and always followed by a more respectable Welsh political genius, David Lloyd George: never neglect your constituency. Humphreys often carried large sums himself, just as often under an alias or wearing a disguise, to insure that a congressman in Washington or a state senator or a colleague received his reward discreetly. But no one could lay a finger on the cash or on him. Certainly it would be foreign to him to involve any city but Chicago in any affairs by which he could be arraigned. He just didn't know enough policemen or politicians or judges in other American cities to feel the security that home gave him. To be tried in a New York court would, therefore, have been particularly disagreeable for him, offending his principles more profoundly, perhaps, than those of his colleagues. His longstanding Capone ally, Frank the Enforcer Nitti, for example, would scarcely be as sensitive.

Or so it might have been thought. Yet as soon as he was indicted in New York, Nitti—who had killed so many to maintain Al Capone's power, who once had had a police bullet rattling around in his head—shot himself. (The British writer Kenneth Allsop, in *The Bootleggers,* reports a rumor that Nitti had been murdered and his body found in a ditch, but the prevailing view is that Nitti's death was suicide.) Why it should have happened is not clear. One school of thought is that Nitti was still depressed at the death of his wife in 1940: he had appeared in court with Humphreys in the Double Jeopardy Trial wearing a black suit and black tie. Another is that he simply could not face going to prison. How could the publicly recognized leader of the Outfit go to jail, and on a charge that was, relatively, of such small import?

For the Camel, Nitti's suicide created difficulties greater than the fact that so many of the mob leaders were likely to be in jail for a long time. Humphreys had spent some time—had even done time—to create an understanding whereby Nitti was treated as Capone's inheritor, as chairman. The public knew him; the law-enforcement officers knew him. In partnership they had prospered, had used the past decade wisely to move away from mere slaughter in the streets to less evident but more secure business. No doubt there were times when they reminisced about the twenties, talked about the days when they would swing mayoral elections with the polemics of the machine gun and the persuasive arguments of the pineapple bomb, throwing acid along with ideological confusion—except that by many accounts, Nitti was not much given to talking. He just granted agreement with Capone and then Humphreys. Who would replace the Enforcer?

More immediately, how long would Ricca, Campagna, Rosseli, Gioe, and the rest be put away? The indictment was long and comprehensive. Essentially, though, it first repeated the charges on which Browne and Bioff had been convicted: demanding money from the Hollywood studios and "restraining and impeding interstate distribution and exhibition of motion pictures." And then there were charges of malpractice in the IATSE union, among them that 2 percent "tariff" imposed on members for the benefit of the boys in Chicago.

Those boys were found guilty as charged and sentenced to ten years in prison. And there was much relief that, at last, the Capone gang was destroyed. Al Capone, its founder, was now a vegetable, near death in Florida. Syphilis, caught in one of his own Cicero brothels, had reached his brain. Nitti was dead. The rest were inside—never, polite society had it, to resume their sway.

One man in Chicago, far from any jail, shared neither the spirit of rejoicing nor the despair. The Camel, as was his wont, was considering the landscape on the other side of the hill and how its contours could be used to his and the Outfit's advantage. He soon evolved a gambit that was to create quite as much fury in the United States as the jailing of his friends had created delight.

11

The disease as epidemic

Father did not have a great respect for politicians because he knew that he could control them. He even knew Harry Truman and at one time Mother and I were in Washington and Harry Truman showed us around. He became President of the United States shortly afterward.

—Llewella Humphreys, in conversation, 1983

What physicians say about disease is applicable here: that at the beginning a disease is easy to cure but difficult to diagnose; but as time passes, not having been recognized or treated at the outset, it becomes easy to diagnose but difficult to cure. The same thing occurs in affairs of state; for by recognizing from afar the diseases that are spreading in the state (which is a gift given only to the prudent ruler), they can be cured quickly; but when they are not recognized and are left to grow to the extent that everyone recognizes them, there is no longer any cure.

—Niccolò Machiavelli, *The Prince*, 1532

In Humphreys's day, after Capone, the Outfit in Chicago always had a corporate structure—and I want to debunk those myths in the movies like the Godfather and the Cosa Nostra: that's all bunkum. In Chicago we

125

had every ethnic group—except minority types. We had no blacks: the gentlemen were not in favor of equal opportunity. So there would be ten people on the board of the Outfit and Humphreys would have the floor more often than anybody else. Accardo would be the chairman, Guzik the vice-chairman and Humphreys would be the president.

—Art Petaque, *Chicago Sun-Times*,
in conversation, 1983

With Nitti dead and the others in jail for who knew how long, the Outfit considered how best to present themselves, both to each other and to the world. Humphreys, at the age of forty-four, was now the important figure among the survivors of the twenties battles. Anthony Accardo was seven years younger; so was Joseph Aiuppa. Jake Guzik, though older, took orders: the Outfit was wise enough not to give its accountant power. None of these was anxious to seize the limelight. There was also Paul Ricca's position to be considered, as the senior man inside.

Among the younger men there was one whom Humphreys is held to have encouraged in this awkward period, in Mike Royko's words, "an unknown semi-literate until Humphreys made him a well-known semi-literate." This was Sam Giancana, who was to want to be known as the leader and to infuriate his mentor by his ostentation. Giancana had been charged with three murders before he was twenty and was to be shot down himself, ten years after Humphreys had died of a heart attack. The second to be advanced was Joey Glimco, a more senior if obscure figure whom the Camel is thought to have introduced to his friend Jimmy Hoffa. Certainly Glimco became the boss in Chicago of Hoffa's important Teamsters' Union and the city's taxicabs. (One story goes that the taxi drivers tried to break away and join with men working the river and Lake Michigan. Hoffa then asked if they thought their taxis would float and had many thrown into the Chicago River.)

If the gang seemed in trouble in 1943 and 1944, the Welshman was observed by friends and family to be cheerful. He was at the height of his profession. The Second World War was being fought far from Chicago. He traveled around America more than he had been accustomed to do. He proposed to buy a house in Florida across the water from Cuba so that he could more easily go deep-sea fishing, which was an enthusiasm of his. "I used to go fishing with him," his daughter told me: "Because he was such a busy man, if I wanted to spend a lot of time with him, I had to do the things he loved doing, and he loved deep-sea fishing. I used to do all the things with him that a son would have done. I used to go hunting with him, too."

Her mother by this time was playing a unique part in the transactions of the Outfit. No other woman, before or since, has been privy to the secrets of the mob. Her unusual memory enabled her to keep their financial transactions in her head. Nothing was written down: Mary Humphreys would simply remember. And even though all those other "gentlemen" were unfortunately in the cooler, Hollywood was still available to the charming Camel and his family.

He also began looking for land in Oklahoma, for a hunting lodge where he could both shoot the wild animals of the territory and enjoy his interest in birds, exotic in that otherwise uncelebrated state. He was determined to build his own house and he did. It still stands, modest, with a small porch, crowded by the trees he planted, its carpentry—hickory and American oak—sound, even expert in the carved chairs. The countryside around was, when I was there, dry, red and dusty, undulating, the rough roads marked by shanties where poor Indians lived. (Mrs. Humphreys was part Indian: her daughter has recently married one.) Winter brings snow and damp cold. There are three small oil wells on the estate that looked to be self-operating. At night the mountain lions and coyotes keep you awake until their noise becomes familiar. The Camel was much taken by the fact that many of the bolder bank robberies conducted by Bonnie and Clyde had taken place only a few miles down the road, but thought the pair stupid to have been caught. He seems to have had no romantic Celtic instinct for self-destruction however much he might have wished, in his heart, to resign from his criminal trade.

His travels, it soon became clear, were not always so uxorious, familial, and innocent. Who knows which alias he used? Lewis Hunt was one; indeed, many of them had the initials L. H., probably because it was useful to have those matching the initials he was christened with and used on his lugguage. Quite where he traveled by train is uncertain: the journalists in the Loop, when the new drama developed, guessed St. Louis, Kansas City, maybe Los Angeles—certainly Washington to see Vice-President Truman, who was so delighted to meet the Humphreys family. Not that it was quite clear why the Camel should be so friendly with former Senator Harry S. Truman: the latter had nothing to do with Chicago. On the other hand, the Kansas City Democratic boss Prendergast and his machine, which had elected Senator Truman, had behaved in the Chicago mode, had emulated its wide-open style in the twenties, had encouraged jazz as much as the Chicago speakeasies ever did. Even so, the relationship had an unlikely air about it in an America where the separate city-states had, traditionally, seldom concerned themselves with each other.

When the storm broke in Washington in August 1947, and Americans began to be aware that Machiavelli's "disease" was truly abroad in the land, Humphreys was elsewhere—indeed, was occupied in conjuring up a new criminal virus in Nevada in his usual insouciant manner that was, as usual, to lead to his own survival and the murders of his better-known associates. The Loop aficionados, when the curtains were lifted, could detect that Humphreys did not need President Truman's help to produce this new drama, even if it did brush the White House. The evidence was that he had fixed it in his own home territory, the Democratic First Ward of Chicago, in the Loop itself.

The 1947 storm broke over the release from jail, on parole, of the Chicago mob after serving only three years of their sentences. The public was incredulous. How could this be? Hadn't this sinister bunch of hoods been put away to break the corrupting powers of the Outfit? And forever, at that? Only six months before, in February, Al Capone himself had been buried in Chicago, four of his old comrades (Humphreys among them) with the family at the graveside. So why should the Justice Department in Washington decide to allow Ricca, Campagna, Gioe, Rosseli, and the rest to emerge from their appropriate prisons in Kansas and Missouri and walk free? It was unheard of for convicted felons to be allowed out after serving less than a third of their sentences. Why make an exception for gangsters? Why, indeed?

The Justice Department had heard many pleas. Little New York Campagna, for example, a man who had once surprised Chicago by pulling a gun on the police chief at his head-quarters, was supported by the Catholic priest Father M. A. Canning:

> I have known Campagna and particularly his family for fifteen years. There are three young daughters just growing to womanhood. One of them is a student at Rosary College. His boy Joe was in the Air Corps and was quite a hero just when his father was going to prison. They promised me with tears in their eyes that he would be a good citizen if he was let out.

Father Canning's supplications and those of the presidents of trucking, construction, and minor newspaper companies in Chicago were not, in the enraged public response, thought to carry as much weight as the lawyer who appeared for the hoods. He was none other than the former campaign manager for President Truman when he had been running for the Senate: a St. Louis lawyer named Paul Dillon. The president's Republican opponents grew almost demented when they further discovered that Attorney Dillon had also defended John Nick and Clyde Weston—as it happens, at Murray Humphreys's request—when both were IATSE union officers in St. Louis and were caught thumping movie theater owners in 1939.

The House of Representatives decided to form a committee to investigate this supposedly unprecedented scandal, the first of many such helpless, solemn inquiries. The parole decisions were to have serious consequences for American society; were to change a nation's understanding of itself, for those who cared to face its implications; were to promote cynicism more publicly; were to show that gangsters were part of the Federal Union; and, in an odd way, were to demonstrate that, after a war in which the nation had fought together, there was a fresh genuine connection between its distant cities and states, if only because corruption united them. Chicago spoke to Washington and Washington answered: Yes. In the meantime the comedy associated with the hoods' release occupied as much space in print and broadcasting as concerns about Soviet policy, about Winston Churchill's concept of the Iron Curtain, about the Marshall Plan. How could any schemes of Moscow compare with the achievements of Chicago?

Mayor Kennelly and Chief of Police Prendergast warned the freed gangsters to keep away from their old stamping-ground. Said the mayor: "We don't want any except law-abiding citizens in Chicago. I have directed my policemen to pick these men up whenever they see them in the streets." Ricca and Campagna responded by saying that they intended to be gentlemen farmers, far from the Loop. D'Andrea thought he might become a steel salesman.

The House of Representatives committee was to dance to the Outfit's tune as cheerfully as to any jazz played by the Mezzrows, Armstrongs, Beiderbeckes, or Goodmans in the hoods' haunts at home. Republican congressmen Hoffman from Michigan and Busby from Illinois, who knew quite well what was going on in the famous First Ward in the Windy City, who were familiar with the history of the Bath and Hinky Dink and their faithful heirs, did all they could to reveal it. They rearrested Campagna and Ricca and D'Andrea for breaking parole by resuming their old work. It did no good. They complained that the hoods had made a deal with the IRS on their illegal earnings, paying in some cases only a quarter of a million dollars when they owed a million. The IRS wearily suggested that half or even a quarter of a loaf was better than no bread at all; and anyway, the U.S. Supreme Court had ruled that "embezzled funds are not subject to income tax." Did extorted funds meet that proviso?

In 1950 the United States Senate reluctantly turned its head toward the scandal of the mob's parole and its implications. Senator Estes Kefauver, who had expressed his concern as a young lawyer in Tennessee at a possible tie-up, as he put it, between organized crime and politics, became Chairman of the Senate Crime Investigating Committee, and between May 1950 and May 1951 traveled the States interrogating witnesses. He discovered little from the Chicago heavies who had been house-trained by Humphreys. But what some of the Outfit's helpers let slip astonished him and his Counsel, Rudolph Halley.

In passing, the committee had condemned the parole given the mobsters, granted "against the recommendations of the prosecuting attorney and of the judge who had presided at their trial. In the opinion of this committee, this early release from imprisonment of three dangerous mobsters is a shocking abuse of parole powers." Its colloquy with the lawyer who helped the gangsters to arrange their tax payments to meet the government's demands equally incensed the committee.

Eugene Bernstein had been an Internal Revenue officer. He studied law in his spare time and acquired a law degree. From time to time he acted as a lawyer for Murray Humphreys and, through him, for Accardo and Guzik. He had never acted for the imprisoned Ricca or Campagna until, mysteriously, he was called in to settle their tax affairs and so help along their release from jail. He began to make trips to Leavenworth Prison in Accardo's company to see the hoods, having, he claimed, met Accardo by chance. It seemed the mobster just walked into his office one day and offered to help settle the matter of Ricca's and Campagna's taxes.

> COUNSEL HALLEY: It just doesn't sound like something I can visualize . . . Who walks in but a notorious gangster, and he tells you, I am the man and you accept that without checking back?
> BERNSTEIN: I never knew Mr. Accardo to be a notorious gangster, sir, at that time, nor do I know him to be a gangster now.

Bernstein, with Accardo's help, was able to persuade the reluctant gangsters that they had to pay some taxes. A settlement was reached and the money paid—although the lawyer testified that he never knew where the money came from. Strangers would just drop by at his office and leave cash with his secretary, some $190,000 in all. In the course of his evidence to the commission, Eugene Bernstein made what Senator Kefauver called a "spirited defense" of Murray Humphreys, claiming that the Welshman had been "forced" out of a legitimate laundry business because of "political activities."

> COUNSEL HALLEY: What do you mean, political activities?
> BERNSTEIN: I mean, because he tried to go into legitimate business and was not permitted to.
> COUNSEL HALLEY: Why not?
> BERNSTEIN: Just because of the newspapers and other people that kept pushing him around.

Senator Kefauver and his colleagues were surprised by this view of Murray the Camel as a pathetic, put-upon businessman striving for respectability. But many of the opinions expressed by Attorney Bernstein, the ex-Revenue man, seemed to take them aback. For example:

> BERNSTEIN: The word "gangster" has a different connotation to me than it may have to other people. A gangster is an individual who by means of force, duress, obtains sums of money. If you and I go out and do certain things legally, and place funds in his possession without duress, at our own direction, and he does something with that, that would not be gangsters. Gangsterism is a very definite form of violence.
> COUNSEL HALLEY: A gangster is a man who belongs to a gang, isn't he?
> BERNSTEIN: Then you and I are gangsters. . . .
> HALLEY: What gang do you belong to?
> BERNSTEIN: We belong to the human race. We belong to a political party. That may be a gang.

The granting of paroles to the gentlemen of the Outfit had

one small effect in Chicago. When the congressmen discovered that money had been at the root of their release, that members of the Democratic party in the Chicago First Ward had "reached" people empowered to grant parole, that some half a million dollars had been made available, the wise men of the First Ward, guided by the Camel, made some changes in response. Peter Fusco, their head, was thought to be embarrassed that one of his sidekicks had been named as a man who passed the bribe. Fusco went to Washington as a national officer of the Plumbers Union and was replaced in the Loop by Frank Annunzio, soon to be appointed State Director of Labor by Governor Adlai Stevenson.

For Murray Humphreys all this commotion had been the preoccupation of two years ago. He had moved on, carrying with him the perception that nothing was now impossible, that Washington was not all that far away—more, that he had once again astonished his colleagues, so much so that he need never again witness anything horrible in the course of his business. It had been a long, long time since he had shot anyone. He was certain he would never need to, whatever other people might do.

12

Vegas, the Senate, and Eisenhower

[The great man] knows he is incommunicable: he finds it tasteless to be familiar; when one thinks of it he usually is not. When not speaking to himself he wears a mask. He rather lies than tell the truth; it requires more spirit and will. There is a solitude within him that is inaccessible to praise or blame, his own justice that is beyond appeal.

—Nietzsche, *The Will to Power*

I went into the room [in 1952] and there were four gentlemen of the Outfit there with my father and another man. One of the gentlemen said to me: "What do you think of Dwight D. Eisenhower?" I said I'd vote for him if I could, to be the next President of the United States. The man next to me said: "Thank you very much, young lady." It was General Eisenhower. I felt very small but I hadn't recognized him without his uniform. . . . Five men there in a room in Chicago decided who was going to be the next President of the United States.

—Llewella Humphreys, in conversation, 1983

For decades the Outfit had made money from illegal gambling in Chicago, and such profits as escaped them usually went, one way or another, into supporting the Democratic party machine in the city. The cash might not go directly into party coffers, but more often into the pockets of those whose job it was to bring out the vote, or to dishonest cops: all contributions were welcome. Murray Humphreys had become more and more impressed at the fashion in which it was easier to make money out of respectable booze than it had been, violently, in Prohibition days.

The manner in which he had divided up legitimate business with Joseph Kennedy in gin, whisky, and beer created, in his mind, a precedent. He now seldom saw the former Ambassador to the Court of St. James, although he did a few times take his wife and daughter to meet the old man and his sons, Jack and Bobby. (He thought, according to Llewella, that Joe Kennedy dominated the children too much; they were growing up "wimps.") With his usual clarity of analysis and consequent action, which with hindsight seems so obvious, Humphreys considered that the next human weakness to be legalized must be gambling. It was just as well for the United States that the Camel had moral objections to exploiting narcotics and prostitution. Or perhaps not.

The choice of the state of Nevada as the territory for the experiment might not have seemed wise. It was far from everywhere, except California. However, it had the virtue that no mobs were established. Flying was becoming fashionable. Given the Outfit's command of night clubs and restaurants in Chicago, and Humphreys's continuing role in the Hollywood unions, it shouldn't be difficult to lay on entertainment of the highest quality in the Nevada desert. More, Humphreys had so many hundreds of thousands of dollars to invest, to launder somehow, that building a new city or two could prove a useful front; and when had anyone gone broke catering to human folly? A persuasive factor was that there didn't seem to be any other state in the U.S. that would lend itself so easily to creating a safe, legal haven for the gambler.

The FBI now believes that the Camel went to Los Angeles in

The birthplace at Carno in mid-Wales of Murray Humphreys' father. A depression in agriculture towards the end of the nineteenth century led many Welsh to migrate. The small farmhouse was named Y Castell (the Castle) because it commanded the valley. The name seems to have encouraged patrician traits in the family.

Left: Murray's parents, Welsh-speaking Brian and Ann. The mother was a clever dignified woman, the father given to using his son's money to gamble. Brian Humphreys' brother became a Justice of the Peace in Wales. The parents appear, as here, in many of Murray Humphreys' home movies.

Below right: Humphreys, the youngest child, remained fond of his brother and sisters, so much so that he placed his older brother, Ernest, in the cinema business to facilitate its corruption.

The beautiful child Llewelyn Morris Humphreys, as he was originally called, contemplates the beginning of the twentieth century in Chicago.

At the age of sixteen Humphreys re-christened himself 'Murray' in honour of a judge who had befriended him, impressed by the young newspaper seller's spirit and intelligence. Many young Chicagoans, like Humphreys, could supplement their income by fraudulent voting for the Democratic machine run by 'Hinky Dink', an alderman. He paid three dollars a vote. There was also burglary, for which Murray Humphreys was arrested in 1916.

Humphreys' wife Mary Brendle was half Irish and half Cherokee. Her mother had survived the 'trail of tears' when the United States government marched the Cherokee into the wastes of Oklahoma. Her business acumen led to her being the only woman privy to the Outfit's finances.

Humphreys' elegance was celebrated and became more marked in the late Twenties when he became Al Capone's agent in corrupting laundry management and trade unions. His jokes about 'laundering' money, about people being taken to the cleaners, were thought to be original. 'Vote early and vote often' was his advice to Chicago's electorate.

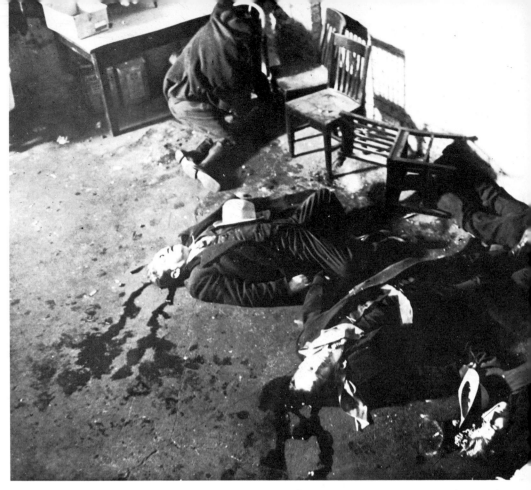

The St Valentine Day Massacre of 1929 remains the most notorious of the Outfit's m
that Capone was intent on killing a rival, Bugs Moran, out of rage at a double-cross i
arrived late. The man who most benefited from the massacre was Murray Humphrey
was his only serious rival in the laundry 'rackets'. The murders took place only a few
birthplace.

Below left: The fact of being crooked always sparked his wit. When he built his daugh
so designed it that it, too, was crooked. This plaque hangs in his Oklahoma house.

Below right: According to the FBI Humphreys was the first person to advise mobsters
Amendment. This and other legal stratagems account for much of the awe and fury h
Attorney-General Robert Kennedy. This plaque, also hanging in his Oklahoma house

Humphreys attracted an unusual number of nicknames. In public he was known mostly as the 'Camel' or 'Murray the Hump', the latter from his surname, the former deriving from the latter. His friends usually knew him as 'Curly' from his fine head of hair. 'Moneybags', the 'Clever Hood', 'Einstein of the Mob' were other journalistic terms.

Received opinion is oze war. But Moran ne of those killed om Humphreys'

all garden house he

the Fifth ed, especially from wife's favourite.

One of Humphreys' handguns which the author held in his hand. There are three notches in the butt. There is no record of how many murders Humphreys committed in the gang wars since he was never charged with any.

When Murray Humphreys asked his daughter Llewella whom she would
like to come and entertain at her Graduation from High School, she asked
for the young Frank Sinatra. He came. Most other of the great American
entertainers would have been just as happy to oblige.

Humphreys seldom
appeared in his own
films since he did not
regard them as frivolous
home movies, but as
properly crafted works.
He would draw titles
for them and give
thought to the
soundtrack. Filming the
island of Alcatraz,
where many of his
colleagues, including
Capone, were
incarcerated, he used
the tune The Gang's All
Here.

Humphreys' final public appearance — the day before his death in 1965 — was to sign a bond granting him bail. He turned to the TV reporter, Jorie Lueloff, who asked him for his comments on the new predicament he found himself in. His answer — that he thought her a very pretty girl — delighted his audience.

Murray Humphreys' daughter Llewella (or Luella) became a concert pianist because her father had said he would like her to be one. She gave three concerts with the Rome Symphony Orchestra and then retired. She was married, for a while, to the Italian actor Rossano Brazzi. Today she lives mostly in Oklahoma.

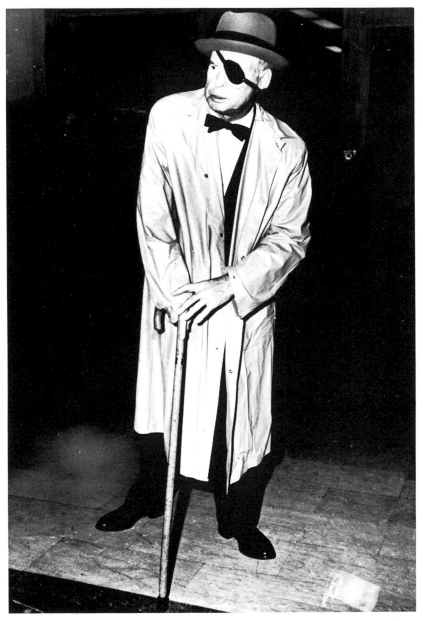

In his fifties Humphreys was persuaded to answer a subpoena demanding his presence before a Federal Grand Jury in Chicago to discover what he knew about organised crime in the United States. He astonished the court by appearing as a lame, shabby, half-blind inarticulate. He was excused, left the court and once outside, threw away stick and eye-patch and skipped through the bars of Rush Street buying drinks for cronies. He seldom drank himself.

1946 with the prominent New York gangster Benjamin "Bugsy" Siegel. William Roemer, the agent who pursued the Camel, told me: "He then switched to Las Vegas from Los Angeles in 1947 and 1948, at the very beginning, just when Las Vegas was getting started. He offered his counsel, as usual. He made his investments on behalf of the Chicago Outfit. But he did more than that. Because of his leadership in organized crime throughout the country, he advised all the gangsters throughout America on their investments, but of course, his loyalty was always to Chicago."

Humphreys was soon to be supported by Sam Giancana, by John Rosseli, once the latter had been paroled prematurely, and by Meyer Lansky. The notoriety of the others became universal, and many singers and actors, presidents and trade union leaders became embroiled in gossip about connections with them. Humphreys, although part-owning two of the most glamorous hotel casinos, did not figure in any gossip.

The Outfit's role and profit in Nevada being established, Humphreys returned to Chicago where he was quickly involved, as anonymously as ever, in charity work and high politics. Siegel, Lansky, and, soon, Giancana could handle the gambling. The Camel seems not to have concerned himself directly in the Outfit's expansion to Cuba, to Beirut and, almost, to Teheran. (Giancana is held to have messed up the negotiations with the Shah.)

Humphreys, it was discovered when he died, had always given large sums of money to good causes. Such generosity is not unusual among the rich in America; what is unusual (and made Humphreys, in the opinion of many, unique) is that he never set his gifts against taxes. Those puzzled by this purity have wondered if his behavior was due to his not wanting to attract notice to his tax position. But that argument does not stand, since he always declared some income, however small a percentage it might have been of his true rewards, to the authorities. Nietzsche offers another possible explanation in *Beyond Good and Evil*: "The noble man also helps the unfortunate not (or scarcely) out of sympathy, but rather out of an impulse produced by the superabundance of power." It may be that the Camel was troubled by guilt, or that he just liked to help. He certainly never spoke of seeing himself as Robin Hood.

For years he had been involved in raising funds for a camp for poor children in Chicago in which his former defense attorney, now a congressman, Roland V. Libonati (he of the riotous victory in 1930) had an interest. Even in 1960 the FBI was reporting that Humphreys was leaning on the Teamsters' Union asking for money for this camp, reminding them of how much Libonati had helped them in Washington. In 1951, however, Humphreys conceived a bold fund-raising scheme. He had seen to it that the relationship between Chicago, Hollywood, and Las Vegas was close. Therefore he would ask those entertainers common to all three places if they would care to offer their services for the "Night of Stars" in Chicago.

Since the charity was designed mainly to help Italian-American children, the arrangements might more properly have been left to the Italian members of the Outfit—Accardo, Ricca, Giancana, and their juniors. But they were lying low as were for much of the time, the equally senior but non-Italian Gus Alex and Jake Guzik. Senator Estes Kefauver's committee investigating organized crime was still wrestling with the Parole Affair: someone, if not the whole mob, was sure to be indicted. It was true that Humphreys's record had been read out to the Senate Committee in Washington in June 1950 by V. W. Paterson, but the Camel was behaving with the air of a man who knew something the others did not.

So here was this sentimental occasion, the Night of Stars. How to present it? The ideal place was Chicago Stadium, holding tens of thousands of people. Bold though Humphreys might be, he could scarcely—either alone or in the company of Giancana, Accardo, and the rest—approach City Hall and ask permission to hire the stadium. Not even Chicago's City Hall could hand over its pride and joy to the Outfit. Hinky Dink and the Bath might have managed it half a century earlier, but this was a big town now and the world was a smaller place: the word would get around. The answer was simple: the First Ward would arrange it. John D'Arco and Frank Annunzio were friendly. They could arrange it through the Democratic party and City Hall.

And so it came to be that the people of Chicago, in 1951 and in the following two years, had glorious concerts at which Jimmy Durante, Frank Sinatra, Tony Martin, Bob Hope, Dean Martin, Tony Bennett, and many more of the most celebrated of entertainers performed. If anyone turned down an invitation, the names have not been recorded. In the real world, the origins of the occasion were known.

The proceeds were handed over to the camp for the poor. There were no rake-offs. The members of the Outfit invariably maintain that in their dealings away from "work" they were honest men. In "work," a different kind of ethic might obtain.

Art Petaque, a scholar with first-hand experience of the field, and a man scornful of the movies and other fictional representations of "The Mafia," defined it to me as follows: "Anyone who attempts to burglarize or attempts to hold up or abuse in any way a crime syndiate member is marked for death—though sometimes they are given a warning, depending on the circumstances. But usually what will happen is that they will be killed first, and the warning will be the killing. The word is then spread as to the reason for the death."

The same warning is given to anyone offering information to police, FBI, or Internal Revenue. The inability to recognize that there might be a common, benign ethic available both in business and in private life is by no means peculiar to the gentlemen of the Outfit or even to American business.

Certainly the gentlemen grew angry when they came to believe that their good works had been mocked once in Chicago.

At the same time as they were organizing the "Night of Stars," Llewella Humphreys told me, her father and his friends decided to spend millions of their own dollars on an act of charity. They would build a model block of apartments and donate them to the city so that a few people, anyway, could move from the slums in which they themselves had been brought up. The apartments were built, but very soon it became evident that the work had been shoddy: the materials were poor and incompetently used; the roofs leaked; the plumbing didn't plumb; the buildings became unsafe. The Outfit was, word of mouth had it, playing a cruel trick: weren't they ripping off enough already?

Such remains the received account in Chicago of what happened in 1952. I tried out the story on my friend Studs Terkel, the chronicler both of the city and of the rest of blue-collar United States. His books *Hard Times, Working,* and *Division Street: America,* recording his conversations with his fellow countrymen, are necessary reading to try to begin to understand the place. In the small company at his seventy-third birthday party in 1983 in the L'Escargot restaurant in his home city, I raised the matter: Studs would know what the people of Chicago remembered of the affair. He recalled it as a mob fiasco. I then passed on the version Llewella Humphreys had given me: he was astonished.

The story really was about the Governor of Illinois, Adlai E. Stevenson, a Democrat. He was hoping to be—and succeeded in being nominated as—the party's candidate for the presidency in November 1952. Chicago was a Democratic stronghold. In 1948 there had been surprise that the crowd of ruffians in charge of the Democratic machine in the city, in Cook County, should have proposed Adlai Stevenson as governor since he was a man celebrated for intellect, charm, and wit, and was a known liberal. Cynics had it that they expected to lose the election and wished to enjoy a worthy, even distinguished image without suffering the practical consequences of enlightenment. However, there he was, the nominee to succeed the Democratic President Harry S Truman and soon to be admired by liberals in Europe for his varied qualities.

The Republicans had nominated General Dwight D. Eisenhower, hero of war and peace, a strong candidate but, given the power of the Democratic machine in important states, not a guaranteed winner. That machine was nowhere stronger or more experienced in the ways of voting than in Chicago and, in Chicago, then in the First Ward, where Humphreys quietly held sway.

Llewella Humphreys takes up the tale: "The gentlemen of the Outfit had invested a great deal of money in this scheme. They were doing it from the heart, not for profit. A construction company with which Adlai Stevenson was connected got the contract. The houses were constructed and about a year after the tenants moved in they started crumbling. In other words, everything was sub-par material. They had really cut corners, more than the normal graft. The gentlemen had been going to support Stevenson, but when they found this out, they changed sides. They decided to back Dwight D. Eisenhower. Father went to see him several times about his ideas and certain promises that would be kept. Then, when General Eisenhower met those five gentlemen in Chicago, I was fortunate enough to walk in on the meeting."

That such a story strikes the visitor as credible says much for United States or at least for Chicago politics. It is a serious matter for any candidate to lose such wealth in support of a campaign. In 1960, when the Outfit had returned to the Democrats in order to support the son of their old sparring partner, Joseph Kennedy, without some thousands of dubious votes cast in the First and neighboring wards, John F. Kennedy might well have lost to Richard Nixon. The spirit of the twenties still lived.

Not that this negotiation was Humphreys's only engagement in high politics in the early fifties, which were also his own early fifties; in his age as much as his behavior he was very much a man of the American century. He had appeared before the Senate Committee and astonished it and the public by pleading the Fifth Amendment. He was told he couldn't do that. He maintained he could. He was cited for contempt, then appeared in court, at which point the United States government learned that indeed the Camel could. When the Senate next attempted to break up the Outfit in 1958, while penalizing colleagues Accardo and Giancana, the decision was taken not to bother Humphreys. Why, no one knew. Perhaps they feared he had some new trick up his sleeve that would make them look ridiculous in a fresh fashion.

Those who knew him believe he would have been just as

capable in the majestic surroundings of the Senate on Capitol Hill of the behavior, in 1959, that so awed a grand jury at the district Federal Court in Chicago. He had flown in from Arizona, by his account, or from his $250,000 house in Key Biscayne, Florida. In the latter palace he was known as Lewis Hart, a retired oilman: "A gracious host, serving tall drinks at the swimming pool, chatting amiably about deep-sea fishing, giving to local charities in the manner of a man of affluence." Wherever he had come from and wherever he was going, he presented a strange spectacle to the jury.

He wore a large black patch over one eye, much in the style of another Welsh pirate, Henry Morgan. His raincoat was crumpled and dirty. His shoes were scuffed. His homburg had seen better decades. He shuffled, supporting himself on a walking stick, pausing every few steps to breathe heavily and peer about him. "Veteran court employees," reported Norman Glubok in the *Chicago American,* "and newspaper men, were moved as they contrasted this shell of a man with the Murray Humphreys they once had known, a vigorous and handsome man whose custom-tailored suits were always immaculate."

He was asked a few questions: he croaked the Fifth Amendment a few times. After five minutes the embarrassed court allowed him to leave. He shuffled into the April air, turned into Rush Street, threw away his walking stick, his raincoat, and his homburg, and skipped as blithely as ever from bar to bar to meet old friends. But the picture of the broken man was in every newspaper: the Camel, as one put it, was over the hump, manifestly finished. That he was as busy as ever, and fit, was not reported.

While these antics were being performed, Humphreys had divorced his wife, Mary, and had married Betty Jeanne Neibert, a former tavern dice girl, pretty, and twenty-five years younger than he. He was to leave her after five years and return to his first wife, saying: "There's no fool like an old fool." Before the divorce, his daughter Llewella had moved to Rome to study music. Her father had said that it would be a wonderful thing to be a concert pianist, so she decided that she would try to become one, as much to please him as herself. Learning to play the piano that well, practicing at least eight hours a day, must be one of the rarer forms of filial affection.

Llewella's childhood had been hard though privileged. To balance the riches and usually cheerful spirits at home were the torments at school. Children in class would imitate the sound of a machine gun and say, "Your pop is going to get it next." Police would take her out of school and take her to a distant precinct, hoping thus to discover where her father was. It was a fine thing to have Frank Sinatra come to her small high school graduation party and have his picture taken with each of them. "He was very thin then, and good-looking and very nice." The obverse was the hounding by the press, for all her father's efforts at privacy and disguise. His sense of irony, if endearing, was also confusing—for example, his joke in building her a doll's house in the garden so that it stood crookedly. She changed her name from Llewella to Louella, did become a pianist, and gave three concerts with the Rome Symphony Orchestra. But Murray Humphreys would not travel to Italy out of fear that he would not be allowed to return to America. She soon retired, so he never did hear her play in the concert hall.

13

Gang murder, number one thousand

Anyone, therefore, who will carefully examine the actions of this man [Emperor Severus] will find him a very ferocious lion and a very shrewd fox; and he will see him feared and respected by everyone and not hated by his armies; and one should not be amazed that he, a new man, was able to hold so great an empire; for his outstanding reputation always defended him from that hatred which the common people could have for him on account of his plundering.
—Niccolò Machiavelli, *The Prince*, 1532

Anything my father wanted, he had; but it was given, not demanded. It was given in homage. He had power, absolute power, more than you can find in the big corporations, because he and his people were into every facet of business. And once the old days were over, they didn't have to threaten any more because they had the power. Let's face it, they were respected for achieving the position they had.
—Llewella Humphreys, in conversation, 1983

The statistics of murder between gangs or within gangs in Chicago are not quite reliable. Is it fair to include the girlfriends of hoods shot in the course of revenge? There is general agreement, however, that as 1959 drew to its close, the figure for the past forty years stood somewhere between 990 and 998, a figure that excludes policemen or bystanders. There had been seventeen indictments that came to court. There had been two convictions. The days of savagery, it was understood, were long gone, murder no more the invention of necessity. Commentators were remarking on the staid gait of corruption but, as it turned out, prematurely. Four days before Christmas 1959, Roger Tuohy (see Chapter 8) was shot down and the press, television, and radio of the United States were able to revive for Yuletide study the saga of the Capone days. Murray Humphreys left town for the holidays.

If this assassination of one of the most prominent enemies of Al Capone attracted universal attention, and may be counted as the thousandth, number 999 four months earlier, on August 26, held more importance both for members of the Outfit and for the authorities. On the morning of that day Frederick Evans was struck down by five bullets at the junction of Lotus Avenue and Lake Street. Evans was sixty years old.

He had appeared in court along with Murray Humphreys in the McLane Affair in 1939 (see Chapter 9). Like the Camel, Evans had interests in the laundry business: the Linen of the Week Inc., Western Laundry Service, Infant Diaper Service, the Dust and Tex Cleaning Company and, the largest, the Industrial Garment Service.

He also was part owner of the two hotels in Los Angeles. Three of his safety deposit boxes were found, holding $500,000 in cash. One report has it that a piece of paper was found in his safe on which was written "Total resources $11 million," but it was not clear if this was accountant Evans's private fortune or that of his collaborators.

Frederick Evans was known to be a servant of Murray Humphreys. His death revealed that he also shared some of his companies with Joey Glimco and, further, that Glimco and the Camel were engaged together in several commercial enterprises. There were hidden interests in record and jukebox companies and in importing motor cars. Only four years later did the investigators discover that Glimco and Humphreys had relatives on the payroll of a construction company that received contracts for $4 million from City Hall.

What, then, had disturbed such a long-standing and profitable business relationship, one that also enabled Evans to live as a well-regarded citizen? Or, rather, a citizen who had never been to jail? It could hardly be that along with Tony Accardo, Sam Giancana, and Joey Glimco (but not Humphreys), Evans had been subpoenaed in an inquiry into a bout of roughhousing in the unions.

The answer lay in an investigation being conducted into Teamster Joey Glimco's affairs by the Internal Revenue Service. The IRS was particularly interested in the income from the Industrial Garment Service. The Outfit was sensitive at this time about income taxes, since their colleague, Paul Ricca, was serving ten years in the Terre Haute Penitentiary in Indiana for tax offenses. (The following year, 1960, according to the FBI, Humphreys was to arrange for Congressman Roland Libonati to visit Ricca in jail, with the result that Ricca was to serve only two years of his ten-year sentence.) The Outfit was led to believe that Evans was telling all to the IRS and a little to the FBI about labor racketeering. So he died suddenly. Glimco was the principal suspect but was not arrested; no one was.

For the public the murder of a bureaucrat—the leaden handshake—though distressing as a comment on the affairs of Chicago, lacked glamour. How different the death of Roger Tuohy and the revelations that followed it. Here was a man who had stood up to the fabulous Al Capone himself, who had defied the mob and maintained his own independent bootlegging business all through the fabulous epoch, though four of his brothers were to be shot down. Toward the end of November 1959 he returned to Chicago, paroled after serving twenty-five years of his ninety-nine-year sentence for the kidnapping of Jake "the Barber" Factor. He even published his memoirs, *The Stolen Years*. The book presents the author as a good man, his only crime running booze illegally, which could, in the Twenties, be held to be a public service. It offers an informed view about the assassination of Mayor Cermak when he stood alongside President Roosevelt in Biscayne Park, Florida, in 1933. The fatal bullet was fired not from the gun of an anarchist who was believed to have aimed to shoot the president, but by a member of the Outfit intent on removing a mayor elected as an enemy of the mob.

Of more interest to those survivors of Prohibition in Chicago, whether public officials, journalists, or gangsters, were Tuohy's accounts of the kidnapping for which he was jailed and his pen portraits of the protagonists. He maintained that the Capone mob had framed him; that he, not being a kidnapper, would never have seized Jake the Barber Factor. Factor, therefore, must have been in cahoots with the Capone Syndicate. The Federal Court appeared to support this judgment at his parole. Roger the Terrible Tuohy then proceeded to refer to Murray Humphreys as a "pimp."

Journalists in Chicago, reading *The Stolen Years* in December of 1959 thought this last epithet tactless of Tuohy. It was well known that the Camel grew angry when anyone suggested that he had anything to do with pimping or with narcotics. Art Petaque confirmed this to me in his office at the *Chicago Sun-Times*: these were "no-nos." Mr. Petaque (in 1983) recalled the book especially well since a friend of his helped Tuohy to write it and subsequently blamed himself for the former gangster's death, believing that had it not been written Tuohy might have survived. (Revelations that followed his death made this improbable).

Petaque also recalled that a surprising number of people could remember where Humphreys had been on December 21, 1959, when the men with shotguns met Tuohy as he stepped from his sister's house. The Camel was seen playing a hand of cards at a place on North Clark Street. He was seen at a table in a bar, his usual small whisky in front of him, with friends. (Humphreys always sat at a table, never at the bar, this demonstrating that he was not a drinking man.) He was seen later at the fashionable restaurant, Fritzl's. I was told at L'Escargot that

Humphreys had also been in there that evening, but scholars doubt this. And, lo and behold, who should be dining that night, just down the street at the Singapore, but Jake Factor, no longer "the Barber" but a rich financier from Beverly Hills, who had just flown into Chicago.

Naturally enough, Murray Humphreys was suspected of being responsible for the murder—although no one supposed he would have carried it out himself, having put that kind of dirty work behind him in his youth. A surprising number of people, anyway, were familiar with his alibi. Just as naturally, the publication of Tuohy's book provoked speculation about that kidnapping of Factor twenty-six years earlier. Had it not been the case that Humphreys had been sent by Capone, along with Sam Golf Bag Hunt, Machine Gun Jack McGurn, and Louis Little New York Campagna, to try to negotiate with Tuohy in 1931? And wasn't he the only survivor of that formidable quartet? Odd, too, that Humphreys had been Public Enemy Number One at the time of the seizing—or not—of Factor, Capone by that time being in jail. And hadn't kidnapping been a tactic Humphreys above all was celebrated for practicing?

Delightful as these questions might be to pose, they were not thought relevant to Tuohy's murder. There were many other suspects beside Humphreys, even though he had a particular motive in the libel against him. Rumor was strong that a small dissident group had approached Tuohy on his release from jail to reemploy his talents to break the monopoly power of the Outfit, to give someone else a piece of huge profits being made in America from the Chicago base.

Even had Tuohy survived to enjoy his first Christmas out of jail in a quarter of a century, a new interpretation of events in 1931 offered at the turn of the year would have insured it was his last. The writer and sociologist Saul Alinsky, who had been a member of the Prison Board at Terre Haute in 1960, made startling claims for the gangster and his relationship with Mayor Cermak, claims which were not made in the memoirs. Received opinion had been that the mayor had been elected on a noble platform: he would drive the Capone mob out of Chicago.

He was also supposed to build up the Democratic machine into such a formidable instrument that it was to make corruption endemic and unshakable, but that was not clear at the time.

Saul Alinsky maintained that the true position was different. In the interests of the mayoral election, the candidate had made a deal with Tuohy. Anton J. Cermak would lend Roger the Terrible his police force, in order to launch an attack on Capone, if Tuohy would help in the Mayoral election. This "revisionist" interpretation dismayed Chicagoans who, looking down the dark caverns of the past, had believed that once upon a time they did elect a genuinely reforming soul to City Hall. On the other hand it would explain why Mayor Cermak was shot down standing alongside the Democrat President Franklin D. Roosevelt, whom the Chicago machine had done so much to help elect. Surely President Roosevelt could never have known that his party could disgrace itself with such a deal.

For the Outfit this fresh account, if true, held particular interest. In the gang warfare that followed the election of Mayor Cermak, nearly all the hoods killed were members of the Capone gang; scarcely any of their rivals were shot. At one time Humphreys and Nitti were losing one soldier every day; they suffered only ninety fatal casualties in the two years from 1931 to 1933, and in the latter year the mayor was shot, and Tuohy was arrested for the Factor kidnap.

Did Capone, Humphreys, and Nitti know of the Cermak-Tuohy deal in 1931? And if not, why not? The murder of the mayor, if it was their work, is not evidence of knowledge. It would be sufficient motive that they were excluded from the machine and were still in some confusion at the ending of Prohibition with their new strategy not yet in place. The collapse of their regime at City Hall probably meant that political intelligence was not good. But more conclusive is the argument that, had they known, Tuohy was unlikely to have been framed for a kidnapping; he would have been shot. And it is even more certain that, had they discovered Tuohy still alive in Chicago, once they had heard Saul Alinsky's tale about just how their troops had been shot down in the early thirties, his days would have been numbered.

Tuohy's death was not to trouble Humphreys directly but to have consequences that created difficulties about his income taxes; and the difficulties about taxes were to link him with as nasty a murder as Chicago had known for a long time. The IRS became interested in a stock transaction between the Camel—or Curly, as he was more usually known now—and the former Jake the Barber (now plain John) Factor. In 1960, after Tuohy's murder, John Factor sold life insurance common stock to Humphreys. Factor was attempting to gain control of the First National Life Insurance Company of America. To this end, he was buying shares at $125 each. However, the financier Mr. Factor sold 400 shares to Mr. Humphreys at $20 apiece. A few months later, Mr. Humphreys sold these shares back to Mr. Factor at $125. Mr. Humphreys had therefore made a capital profit of $42,000 without straining himself. What a mysterious transaction, thought the IRS. The FBI also was curious but, as ever, might just as well have banged their heads against a brick wall.

The IRS, like the FBI, continued its researches into the elder statesman of the Outfit. Agents asked him where he had found the money to buy the mansion in Florida, since his income didn't seem to suggest he had been able to raise such a large sum in cash. They were also curious about his interest in a beer company that paid his friend Anthony Accardo (now regarded as the chairman of the Outfit) $75,000 a year in salary. They were not persuaded that he was retired, half-blind, and frail, even if the public had been.

Humphreys was untroubled. He explained that much of the money for the house in Key Biscayne had been given by his new wife, Betty Jeanne, when they had married six years earlier in 1957. To his astonishment, he then discovered that the IRS would not accept his statement. Why? Because his wife's former husband, Irving Vine, had offered to give evidence against him. Vine's first piece of testimony had been that Betty Jeanne could not possibly have $50,000, as Humphreys had reported her gift to be.

Irving Vine in 1963 was fifty-nine years old. Murray Humphreys was sixty-four. His second wife, whom he was soon to leave (although he remembered her, as they say, in his will), was in her thirties. There is no firm evidence that Betty Jeanne had indeed "left" Vine for Humphreys. However, Murray Humphreys was a mogul in the Outfit, the nonpareil. Vine had been only a bit player, always barely making his way on the crumbs from the mighty, but a member of the gang for all that.

Rules that obtained for the highest obtained for the lowest. Therefore there was consternation when it became known that Vine was helping the IRS against the Camel. If it was jealousy, so virulent a form had not before been seen.

When Willie Bioff had squealed in 1943—and even he had not moved against the Camel—he had later been blown to eternity as his reward. The gentlemen of the Outfit called on Irving Vine to consider his position. Murray Humphreys suggested to him that he was being foolish and that no good would come of it. Harm would come of it—especially to Vine.

Whichever strange god Vine was pursuing, he further informed the IRS that his former wife never earned more than $75 a week, sustaining his evidence that she had not saved $50,000 while she was married to him; therefore the famous Murray Humphreys was telling them a pack of lies.

Even after this betrayal, friends high and low continued to visit Vine, urging him to consider his apostasy, these visits being taken as a sign that Humphreys was exhibiting a patience no other chieftain would have shown. Vine refused to listen.

His was to be a dreadful martyrdom. It took place at the Del Prado Hotel in Hyde Park. The hotel was owned by Ralph Pierce, Humphreys's Irish assistant. Humphreys's parents had once lived there, free, in great comfort. Ovid Demaris, in his *Captive City*, had this account of the morning of May 6, 1963:

Rosie Mitchell, a chambermaid, noticed that the door to Room 507 was ajar. After a discreet knock, she stepped into the room, took one look, and stepped right out again, screaming. Homicide detectives found Irving Vine lying on the floor, dressed only in blood-smeared shorts, his mouth and nose sealed with surgical tape, his legs also bound with tape, a shirt twisted loosely around his neck, and a pillow covering his head. Three of his ribs were broken, his face was scratched and his knees bruised, but the real damage was to the lower part of his body where savage tortures had been inflicted with an ice-pick during a period of several hours. Death was due to suffocation, "by person or persons unknown." Police stated they would like to question Humphreys, Betty Jeanne, Gus Alex, Edward Vogel, Nathan "Butch" Ladon, Bernard "Pipi" Posner, and Ralph Pierce, the hidden owner of the Del Prado Hotel. Betty Jeanne remained in Florida; Humphreys vacated his Chicago apartment and successfully avoided arrest by becoming a nomad for a few weeks.

Later, Humphreys was to express his shock at what had happened, the implication being that he was not responsible for the behavior of his troops or, rather, the Outfit's troops; the further implication being that Vine really had to go. Otherwise, where would the Mob be, with satraps running to the IRS? In 1963 this demand for loyalty was becoming more serious than ever; the assaults on the gang by the IRS and the FBI were critically damaging. Indeed, for the past years, since 1958, the Outfit had needed to contend with a new force against them: Robert Kennedy. As counsel to the Senate committee and as attorney general when his brother Jack became president in 1961, Bobby Kennedy had set his sights on the Outfit. Humphreys was a principal target. The Camel found this wry, having been an old rival of the brothers' father and having, as the Chicago mob thought, helped to arrange President Kennedy's election. It was to be a battle to many deaths.

14

The Camel and the
Kennedys

> When Robert Kennedy took action against the Syndicate it was a turning point for my father and the organization, a time of great pressure. Before that, any information that was gleaned was either from the precincts or from a city. They, like a state or a county, or the FBI, had different pieces of evidence. If anyone tried to put all this information together to try to get something on someone it might take a year or two. Bobby Kennedy came along and put a central computer in Washington to which everything went. It really was a problem for the gentlemen of the Outfit. He stepped on some toes, did Bobby Kennedy, and there was a lot of talk about how to remedy the situation.
> —Llewella Humphreys, in conversation, 1983

Had I known more about Murray Humphreys at the time, what would I have done with the knowledge? In May 1963 I was in the Oval Office at the White House with President Kennedy and his brother Robert.* We talked about unemployment in West Vir-

---

*I was there to help to arrange the first live BBC satellite television broadcast between America and the United Kingdom. President Kennedy was awarding an honor to Sir Winston Churchill, whose son Randolph was receiving it on his father's behalf. The pioneer pictures of the ceremony in the Rose Garden arrived perfectly in London. The trunk line carrying my sound commentary broke down.

ginia and Kentucky, where I had just spent a couple of weeks filming. Humphreys, "the brainy hood," I knew of only as an unlikely Welsh legend. But if I had realized that the brothers' father, Joe, had been the Camel's rival in the old days, would I have said anything? Or had I known that Robert, both as a Senate counsel and as attorney general, had a special loathing for the Welshman and had been foiled so often in his pursuit, might I have asked why it was that Humphreys was so elusive when other mobsters had been jailed? Whether the rumor that the Mob had been involved in the Cuban Bay of Pigs fiasco was true? Even that the CIA was looking for its help in assassinating Fidel Castro? What delicate form of words could be found to ask if it were true that Humphreys had invested in the 1960 West Virginia primary where victory was so important to the then Senator John F. Kennedy? And further, that the ten thousand votes whereby Chicago and Illinois swung to Kennedy against Richard Nixon, and so took JFK to the White House, were more or less fraudulently arranged by the master fixer?

In retrospect, it would have been a good time to have raised the subject since the Camel had recently helped to engineer an exceptional coup in Congress through his good friend, Rep. Roland Libonati. On the grounds that the civil rights of citizens—namely, themselves and fellow hoods throughout the nation—were being infringed upon by the wiretapping of the Mob's meetings, the attorney general had been instructed to stop the practice. This was popularly known as the "James Hoffa resolution" since it was partly in aid of Hoffa, the President of the Teamsters' Union and a Humphreys protege, who had complained that Attorney General Kennedy was persecuting him. In a memorable if meaningless phrase, Hoffa had cried at Kennedy: "Sticks and stones may break my bones but words are only yesterday's whispers."

In considering the relationship between the Camel and the Kennedy family, federal wiretaps hearsay, often persuasive gossip, and the evidence of such court appearances as the attorney general could persuade Humphreys to make have to compensate for any direct testimony. The matter is made more complicated because Humphreys, in the relevant period from 1958 to the murder of President Kennedy in Dallas in 1963, had placed Sam Giancana in the limelight. That Giancana's behavior infuriated the Camel is known; nevertheless, in the FBI wiretapping files it is the fatally vain Italian who does most of the enraged shouting against the Kennedys. Humphreys's technique to deal with the FBI's eavesdropping was simple: open the meetings of the Syndicate by announcing briskly that the session had begun and then remove the microphone. He also acquired a telescope that he would train on any agents who were watching out for him. Nevertheless there are wiretap records of some of his deals, especially in Las Vegas, when he was engaged in removing millions of dollars from hotels there in the early sixties.

In 1958 Robert F. Kennedy let it be known that he was determined to attack the Outfit or Syndicate, recognizing that it was a more serious disease in the society even than the Mafia. His particular enemy was Murray Humphreys, followed by Jimmy Hoffa, Anthony Accardo, Gus Alex, and Sam Giancana. Kennedy was then chief counsel of the Senate "Rackets" committee or, to give it its full title, the U.S. Senate Select Committee on Improper Activities in the Labor or Management Field. In turn the mobsters appeared before the Senate committee and pleaded the Fifth Amendment; Hoffa was taken to court, but was acquitted; Accardo was taken to court and convicted of income tax evasion.

Humphreys never even appeared before the Senate committee. Kennedy could not find the means to serve a subpoena on the Welshman. No one is able to explain why this should be.

How could it come about—as in the Hollywood trial—that the one man everyone knew was peculiarly relevant to any rackets investigation in modern times could simply stroll away from a summons to a Senate hearing? In the Hollywood case, it was that he was too much admired by his colleagues to be sold out. Surely it could not be the position that no agent of federal law could be found to carry out so distasteful a task. Was it, perhaps, that he had quite persuaded everyone by his antics in other courts that he was retired or sick, a feeble figure of no account?

This is improbable, since at this time the FBI agent William Roemer was meeting Humphreys frequently in Chicago. Roemer's first meeting with the Camel (see Chapter 1) had impressed the young officer. He had complained about his children being harassed at school by hoods from the Syndicate. Humphreys had listened politely and assured the FBI man that such behavior would stop, proposing that each side behave with courtesy toward the other. Here was the Camel, as ever, conducting himself as if he were some plenipotentiary from a rival state within the state. No doubt that is how he saw his role.

If Humphreys's success, then, in refusing to appear before the Senate committee is inexplicable, it did at least have the consequence of persuading Robert Kennedy to unleash hundreds of phone- and wire-tapping agents in pursuit of the Camel's colleagues. This decision was to embarrass him later when the Director of the FBI, J. Edgar Hoover, let it be known that he had done nothing that Kennedy had not approved of—knowledge the Kennedys' liberal friends did not care for.

Robert Kennedy's rage against the Outfit, both when he was chief counsel and, after January 1961, when he became attorney general in his brother's administration, is a rare and admirable flourish in American life. The question is whether or not he was so determined *because* his father had been a gangster before his wealth carried him as Ambassador to the Court of St. James in London, assuming that the son knew of his father's history in the bootlegging battles of the twenties in Chicago.

It is not given to many families in the Western world for one son to be a president and another an attorney general, intent on jailing a hood who had once sat down with the father in a room in Chicago and carved up the distribution of liquor in a state—once they had stopped throwing bombs at one another. Was there, in Bobby Kennedy's determination, some anguish about his parentage? A desire to expunge the past, a bizarre form of patricide?

The matter becomes more complicated if he was aware of his father's long affair with a Hollywood film star. Would that, in turn, explain his own with Marilyn Monroe? Again, would it all become more complicated for him to discover that his brother the president had taken a girlfriend, arranged by the ubiquitous Humphreys, who had been the lady of the horrible Sam Giancana—to wit, Judith Campbell Exner? It is not surprising that Robert Kennedy seemed like a man possessed. It may also be, as some Americans argue, that Bobby Kennedy was merely carrying out his father's orders: put my old enemies in jail, son.

Another question therefore arises: why should Humphreys have had the Outfit support Senator John F. Kennedy's campaign for the presidency when his brother Robert was so determined to destroy them? Humphreys often expressed privately his dislike of Joe Kennedy, believing him to be an egomaniac. He thought the patriarch had done both John F. and Robert F. harm by seeking to express that mania through their careers. According to his daughter, Humphreys's view of the relationship between parents and children was that it should be an affectionate one in which the parent gently guided and taught the child. He thought Joe Kennedy had terrorized his children into ambition and a passion for fame and money and power. Ergo: the children were weak, were "wimps." That a gangster, celebrated in the rackets and famous among murderers, the very image of a corrupter, should be so accustomed to speaking familiarly in his after-dinner chat of the rulers of the world's most powerful nation, has long ceased to surprise.

THE REASONS WHY the Outfit supported John F. Kennedy have to do with an idiocy about Cuba and common sense about Chicago. The idiocy was Giancana's; the sense, Humphreys's. Fidel Castro's triumph in Havana had caused general distress among the criminal classes in the United States. It was not merely that the senior gangsters enjoyed fishing in the Cuban waters; they owned the brothels and the gambling dens. Suddenly they had been deprived of pleasure and income. What was the government going to do about this grave interference with property and freedom? Surely a God-fearing Washington would reclaim the territory, restore the dictator Batista, and get the girls and the gambling wheels turning again.

Sam Giancana, always active in Cuba and Central America, seems to have been persuaded by rogue elements in the CIA that he could play a heroic role: saving his investments by his exertions and the nation by his example. With a Kennedy in office, son of Humphreys's old sparring partner Joe, Giancana would be the very man. Humphreys was more skeptical, perhaps not seeing himself as a foreign affairs specialist. Giancana was for invading Cuba and killing Castro. But Humphreys was more troubled by a problem at home in Chicago in the First Ward.

There had been a fresh police scandal in Chicago. The Democratic boss, Mayor Richard J. Daley, had barely survived in power in 1959 when the citizens had discovered that practically all his police officers were on the take. The presidential election was in November 1960. Mayor Daley had already abandoned Adlai Stevenson, who was anxious to be the Democratic candidate for the third time. He had supported a fellow Irish Catholic, John F. Kennedy, and swung Illinois behind him.

As Mike Royko devastatingly argues, though, in his biography of Daley, *The Boss,* the Chicago mayor regarded the election of Kennedy as secondary to the local battle. The machine—that engine invented, reinvented, refined, and refueled over the decades by Hinky Dink, the Bath, Kelly, and Nash, with Humphreys so often courteously in attendance, now presided over by Daley—was to have a glorious hour. American commentators had already begun to suggest that radio and television had put an end to the capacity of the Outfit, or even the precinct, to deliver. The public would now be swayed by the image, not by the wardheeler wielding the old devices. But Chicago was not yet done. Humphreys went to work.

Mike Royko, who was later, in his obituary of the Camel (see Chapter 16), to write one of the classic columns in American journalism, considers that the crisis for the machine, the Outfit, and all who lived by these powerful engines of corruption and fortune, was represented by Benjamin Adamowski. This lawyer was the elected district attorney of Illinois. He was a nuisance. He had revealed that when burglaries took place in Chicago, the burglars were often the police. Accustomed as the citizens were to fraudulence among the cops when it came to traffic offenses or the behavior of the courts, there did seem something somehow wrong about the police being burglars. Hard to put a finger on quite what was wrong, but it seemed not altogether right.

Mayor Daley and the Camel saw the matter differently: the offense was the behavior of District Attorney Benjamin Adamowski. He had to be defeated in the November elections, or who knew what else he might discover. Adamowski was standing as a Republican on the same ticket as Richard Nixon. John F. Kennedy was on the Daley ticket.

"Daley has stolen the White House," Adamowski said when he learned that he had lost and that Kennedy had carried Illinois by ten thousand votes. These few votes enabled Kennedy to win enough electoral college votes to make him president. Had they gone the other way, Richard Nixon would have been elected, and Camelot would not have come to the White House. All that romance and glamour would never have been. The Vietnam War might never have been. The Kennedy brothers might never have been assassinated.

After the Kennedy victory and before the new president welcomed Mayor Daley to the White House—"We were the first family invited to the White House," proclaimed the mayor, and why not?—there was an uproar in Chicago. Mike Royko described the course of events once the Republicans and Adamowski had objected to the conduct of the polls:

> Daley's election board soberly announced that it would be glad to conduct a recheck, and it began, one precinct a day. At that pace they would complete the recheck in twenty years. When they stopped stalling, it became obvious that if they hadn't stolen the White House or, more likely, Adamowski's office, it wasn't because they hadn't tried. In 900 precincts in which ballot papers were still used, the recheck caused a switch of ten thousand votes . . . Daley's election board members looked

innocent throughout the limited recheck and blamed it all on
human error, brought on by the fatigue of a long day and
evening in the polling place. They didn't explain why the
human errors consistently benefited Democrats.

The fraud was so obvious that Daley had to permit a special
prosecutor to be appointed to investigate. More than six
hundred polling-place workers and precinct captains were
brought to trial. To assure that the fix would not be put in by a
local judge, a downstate judge was called in to hear the cases.
The downstate judge turned out to be a faithful organization
Democrat, and later most of the charges were wiped out.

The Kennedys, being a Boston-Irish family with an entertaining pedigree in that city's politics, would probably not have
been surprised at the customary Chicago behavior. To win by
one vote is as fine a thing in a democracy as winning by millions.
And if that voter had been dead a long time, or was a horse: well,
it had happened the other way around in Chicago from time to
time. The distinction between Boston or New York and Chicago
was that in the Windy City there was that dreadful tradition of
the vote's often carrying a bullet along with it, that murderous
element that gave a politician, like a gangster, a sense that he
was living on the dangerous edge of things.

In that intoxicating time of John F. Kennedy's inauguration
as president in January 1961, when he seemed to offer in his
rhetoric a youthful hope to a troubled world, it would not have
been seemly to suggest that he had won by votes fixed by a few
unsalubrious elements in the Loop.

Bobby Kennedy was not inhibited. Now attorney general, he
renewed his attack on the Outfit, the Mafia, and the corruption
within government. In his three years in office, reports William
V. Shannon in his portrait *(The Heir Apparent),* he prosecuted

numerous Democratic politicians including two Congressmen,
three State Supreme justices, five mayors, two chiefs of police,
and three sheriffs. One of those convicted was New York State
Supreme Court Justice Vincent Keogh, the brother of Congressman Eugene Keogh, an Administration stalwart on the

House Ways and Means Committee and a personal intimate of President Kennedy.

His father used to say that "Bobby hates like I do." His fervor for justice, however complicated his motive, was to have its effect. The mobsters would not, in the nature of things, step onto a public platform to denounce the new president and his brother, but their associates certainly would when they could. Jimmy Hoffa took the opportunity of his annual Teamsters' Union conference at Miami Beach, Florida, early in July 1961 to let the attorney general know his view.

Murray Humphreys had stopped in at the conference since he happened to be staying at his mansion nearby, using the name Lewis Hart—or was it Harris? He heard the two thousand Teamster delegates cheer his friend Jimmy Hoffa "wildly," as reports had it, and must have taken pleasure in seeing how well that young man he had nurtured in the ways of trade unions and commercial life so long ago had done. Attorney General Kennedy had already lost two cases prosecuting Hoffa for corruption. The London *Economist* reported:

> Few trade union gatherings have received as much attention as the one that the teamsters have just concluded in Miami Beach, Florida. According to Mr. Hoffa, the watchers included the government forces which are still actively pursuing him. Before the convention he charged that more than 150 agents of the Federal Bureau of Investigation were scouring the country looking for any signs of illegality in the choice of delegates or anything else that might be used to prevent him from being confirmed in the presidency, to which he thought he was more than entitled. During the convention Mr. Hoffa warned the delegates that female agents of the government might use their wiles to uncover evidence against him; and later during the proceedings he showed the delegates an electronic listening device which he said had been hidden in a television set to eavesdrop on his conversations.

Later, Hoffa was to go to jail and then to be murdered in

unexplained circumstances, but this day he was expressing not
only the feelings of the meeting but those of the observing
Camel. The Kennedy "buggings" were beginning to be a problem, along with the computer the attorney general had introduced into the Justice Department.

Murray Humphreys, now in his sixties and by his daughter's
account longing to give up his profession, and having suffered a
mild heart attack, had been presented with one of his most
taxing tasks—and by a president he had helped to elect. He was
soon to demonstrate that his genius, that ever sparkling spring
of invention, was not exhausted. In the meantime there was the
question of Cuba and Giancana. The life of the prince is not an
easy one, the demands on his energy and guile being ceaseless,
especially when his company takes the view that a gun can settle
every problem.

Giancana saw the disastrous Bay of Pigs enterprise—in which
a motley mob hastily assembled by the CIA, with or without the
president's support, attempted to retake Cuba, only to founder
in the water—as a serious effort by the Kennedys to repay their
debt to the Outfit that had supported their election to power.
Since Giancana had been engaged in covert negotiations with
the CIA to kill Castro, he could not be blamed for detecting a
connection between his aspirations and those of the president. It
may be that his analysis was correct. Or it may have been, given
the tense hours that subsequently troubled the world when
President Kennedy and Mr. Khrushchev confronted each other
about the Soviet presence in Cuba, that the U.S. government had
preoccupations other than the fate of the Mob's brothels and
gambling houses in Havana. Giancana's opinion was that the
Kennedys had let him down.

The brooding Camel removed himself from these grand questions of state. How was he to prevent the damaging inroads the
attorney general was making on his colleagues and their political and judicial friends? As ever, he addressed himself to the
important question. What exactly was the attorney general
doing? He was intruding on the private conversations of citizens
of the United States, free men whose rights were protected by a
venerable constitution. Was this not a monstrous interference

with the liberty of the individual? Why should he, Llewelyn Morris Humphreys, when meeting colleagues at Schneiders or at the Armory for a meal or drink, or at the Desert Inn in Nevada, have his private conversation overheard? Therefore: Attorney General Kennedy, a member of a family synonymous with liberal thinking, his brother the darling of the high-minded intelligentsia, was an enemy of the rights of the citizens. Something had to be done.

Particularly it had to be done because Anthony Accardo was in jail and a little cross that the Camel hadn't shown his usual skill in keeping him out of so unpleasant and unlikely a place. (The Humphreys view was that he could scarcely be held responsible for friends going to jail on income tax charges; his responsibility was for more serious matters.) Scores of other colleagues were becoming troubled by FBI agents tailing them, surrounding their houses, plaguing their girlfriends, upsetting their travels.

The Camel approached his old friend, Congressman Roland V. Libonati, a man on whose piano he'd laid his gun on that famous night in the wild old days when Libonati was elected to the Illinois State Assembly, the man who had defended him in the even more famous Double Jeopardy trial in 1939. Also, of course, the man the FBI had observed accepting from the Camel a parcel thought to contain greenbacks at the Woodner Hotel in Washington in May 1960, not to mention the same Libonati with whom Humphreys had discussed the parole of Paul Ricca from the penitentiary at Terre Haute. In other words; the faithful "Libby" Libonati. He was an important man in Washington now. Moreover, was he not part of the Chicago machine that had brought President Kennedy to his narrow victory and, along with him, many cars on the gravy train?

It is difficult for those who are not American politicians or gangsters to guess at quite how the conversation went. From what I have heard of Humphreys's tone in his home movies, and from the accounts of his style from those who knew him, it is feasible that he opened his speech, or marching orders, to the congressman with general remarks on the importance of the liberty of the citizen. He may have continued by saying that life was becoming very difficult. Probably he would have told the congressman that some members of the relevant House Judiciary Committee had certain weaknesses, were perhaps beholden in this way or that, perhaps needed cash for their reelection, or whatever. And wouldn't there, anyway, be plenty of enemies of the Kennedys on the committee?

Libonati went to work on his campaign to have a motion accepted by the Democratic majority to "investigate the Justice Department's activities concerning individual rights and liberties as guaranteed by the Constitution and the laws of the United States regardless of the administration in power." The attorney general, furious, warned the Chicago machine that he found Libonati's insolence so intolerable that if their man were to stay in the Congress after the next election, he would have him arrested. Libonati agreed not to run again, but his resolution was passed by the attorney general's own party. Before the matter could be pursued any further, Robert Kennedy was no longer in office. And his brother, the president, had been murdered in Dallas.

American presidents had been assassinated before and attempts have been made since on Presidents Ford and Reagan, but in each case except that of John F. Kennedy it has been reasonable to regard the dreadful deed as the aberration of a self-willed killer. The death of President Kennedy is bewildering. His murder in Dallas is one of the shocking events of the last half of the twentieth century. He was, in his time, the very image of a statesman. That, subsequently, the image may not have been the true man is irrelevant: a politician who can seem to be so for his people and epoch has done enough. His death was seen as a tragedy, the cruel end of a bold, handsome hope.

Seen, though, from the perspective of the Outfit, Kennedy's murder is less surprising. The assumption is general in Chicago that he was killed by agents either of the Syndicate or the Mafia, more probably the former since the Mafia is not held in high repute. In a not altogether mysterious manner, the Kennedys were regarded by the Outfit as a presidential family that belonged.

Belonged to what precisely, is not so clear. Probably to immigrants, associated through Joe Kennedy's bootlegging and Hollywood days with the wild, successful Irish. Therefore there was at best a disappointment, at worst a betrayal, at the failure over Cuba and the even more distressing puritanism of Robert Kennedy. To offer such an interpretation is probably to gloss over the attitude of the hoodlums. Brutally, if they shot him it is because that was their simple solution to every problem.

There is no evidence that the Camel had any hand in the murder of the president or its arrangement, but he seems to have shared the general view that the Kennedys were bound to meet trouble at the hands of the Outfit. The Camel's own concern in his last years was to resume his family life with his first wife and with his daughter. He made little effort to keep the obnoxious Giancana out of jail early in 1965. He reflected, as survivors will, on what fortune it had been that so few of the great and the bad he had worked with were still alive, that he had escaped the bullet and the pineapple. He had not long to live now, but in his last months he was still to demonstrate to his loyal Chicago public that he had some tricks and some wit to offer.

15

Humphreys dies: heart attack blamed

HIS EPITAPH: NO GANGSTER WAS MORE BOLD
—Headline, *Chicago Sun-Times*, November 1965

Humphries died of unnatural causes—a heart attack.
—Mike Royko

When I heard that he was dead, it was like a friend of the family or a relative had passed away. A chapter in my life was ending. I didn't sleep hardly at all that night. I knew that he was a murderer, an extortionist, and an acid thrower and everything. I knew all the bad things. But in the fifty or so contacts that I had with Murray Humphreys, I learned to have a grudging respect for that man, and I knew I was never going to see him again and that saddened me.
—William Roemer, FBI agent, in conversation, 1983

Q: Do you have any comment on your arrest, Mr. Humphreys?
A: My, but you are a very pretty girl.
—Humphreys's last words to a television interviewer, November 23, 1965

The explanations of Murray Humphreys's decision in June 1965 to visit his daughter and first wife at the ranch in Oklahoma rather than appear before the grand jury in Chicago, are contradictory and each in turn contains its contradictions. The family view is firm. He had innocently come to see them. There were a few domestic business affairs to be discussed. He was his usual cheerful self, reconciled to the fact that the state of his heart was not good and that he could have another attack at any time.

Four years later the Chicago columnist, Art Petaque, was to publish a speculation that had haunted the mob after the Camel's death, about the whereabouts of his great fortune. There was supposed to be some $10 million in cash somewhere. His daughter has told me that he certainly did not mention it on this visit, the last time she was to see her father alive.

He appeared to be delighted to be in the house that he had built himself and quite untroubled, both by his fresh income tax trouble over the First National Life Insurance Company stock deal and by the jailing of Sam Giancana. The family was aware of how much difficulty Giancana had created. They maintain that as soon as he heard on the radio that a warrant had been served on him in Chicago—news confirmed when brother Ernest phoned—he left to catch a train from Norman to accept the subpoena sworn at William Roemer's request; that he decided to take the train rather than use his return air ticket, from Oklahoma City to Chicago, since he had calculated it would get him there sooner.

Humphreys himself argued that he had left the telephone number of his lawyer with the FBI—he never answered his own telephone—so that he could be reached any time he was wanted. It was by chance that he gave the wrong number and had offered, instead of his lawyer's, the number of a construction company in Chicago; it was scarcely his fault if that office chose to deny any knowledge of him. Moreover, would he have bought himself a return air ticket if he wasn't intending to return?

William Roemer took—and still takes—a different view. He says that he had good reason to think that Humphreys really was going to stay away from Chicago. The prosecution device whereby Giancana was imprisoned presented Humphreys with an equal difficulty. While infinitely cleverer than the hood he had come to despise, and perhaps because he was so perceptive, he recognized the trap this time of retreating to the haven of pleading the Fifth Amendment that he had invented so long ago. Perhaps the jig really was up.

By this FBI reading, Humphreys had gone to the Norman railroad station rather than use his return air ticket to Chicago not in the interests of speed but rather to rehearse a fresh disguise and leave the country. Wouldn't that provide a motive for a visit to the family, to his old house and hunting and birdwatching ground? Perhaps he even had in mind to retire to Wales. Therefore, the FBI had been fortunate to catch him just in time and arrest him in Norman. Humphreys was shocked at this analysis and furious that he was handcuffed when arrested, like some kind of criminal.

Whatever the truth, when Humphreys appeared in court in his home city he was, to judge from the newspaper reports, in commanding form. His opening gambit was to have his lawyer, Maurice J. Walsh, suggest that the jury was illegal on the grounds that the clerk of the federal court had not called out the names of the jurors as they were drawn. U.S. District Attorney Hanrahan protested that all this was "an abuse of the court's process." Humphreys next offered a petition to quash the subpoena under which he had been ordered to appear. The infuriated Judge Campbell told the Camel: "The grand jury does not have to explain to you why it is going into anything. They are doing what I hope you will do—their duty as citizens of the United States. You are not to argue with them." At which point a woman member of the jury asked Humphreys, "Are you proud, would you be proud, to be an American citizen?" To which he replied that he refused to answer on the grounds that it might tend to incriminate him.

Since Humphreys had been made to post a bond for the huge sum of $100,000 to enable him to be free to live at his opulent apartment in the high-rise Marina Building across the Chicago River from the court, the public, or such public as had failed to escape the August heat, grew convinced that the "brainy hood" was on the same route to jail as the thug Giancana. The detailed development of his questioning had a traditional air about it.

Would the Camel care to explain the significance of a party held with a few surviving Capone colleagues on the anniversary, in 1962, of the St. Valentine's Day Massacre? Why did he see so much of the Democratic Party's First Ward boss, Pat Marcy? He had nothing to say.

Only at one point did Humphreys lose his temper. He was asked if a trip he had made to France in 1963 had anything to do with narcotics. He replied at length, saying he had nothing to do with narcotics and never had. Everyone knew that about him. He did not add that he had been on a European trip, taking in Wales, in the company of both his first and second wives, no doubt judging that to be no one's business. What he did add was that if he was going to be asked any more questions about narcotics he doubted if he would return to talk to the grand jury.

Mostly, though, Humphreys beamed at the court as he had that day twenty-six years earlier when the case against him in the McLane Affair collapsed, and for much the same reason. He had his attorney, Maurice Walsh, ask the judge whether the object of this appearance was to follow the precedent set by Giancana whereby it was "an attempt to create a situation for the offense of contempt and have him incarcerated." Judge William Campbell called U.S. Attorney Edward Hanrahan before the bench and asked him if such was the government's intention. Hanrahan replied: "No, it is not my present intention." And so the $100,000 bond was canceled without the prosecution's putting up a fight, the grand jury was dismissed, and Humphreys strolled away. Could it really be magic? All done by mirrors?

This unexpected development—although, given the Camel's history, it should not have surprised the FBI as much as it did—might suggest that the Humphreys version of the flight into Oklahoma was correct. What did he have to fear from the grand jury? He must have known in June that he would not, in August, meet Sam Giancana's fate and finish up in jail. After all, he and the rest of the Outfit hierarchy were as fed up with

Giancana as the government was. The grand jury would surely believe his account, too, of his trip to see his family as, indeed, it appeared to. Surely even the maestro of corruption, the incomparable manipulator of public officials, couldn't have managed such a "fix" in just five weeks. Assurances must have been given earlier.

Whatever was the case, the indefatigable FBI agent Roemer, even if baffled by this latest instance of Chicago's cultural peculiarities, remained determined. The children in the parks might still, after the most recent city police scandals, play the new game of "cops and cops," the Feds were different.

On November 23, 1965, William Roemer decided that he had enough evidence to swear out another warrant for the arrest of the sixty-six-year-old statesman of the Outfit. He described to me the events of the day and their consequences:

> I had developed certain evidence after the grand jury hearing that I knew would prove that Murray Humphreys committed perjury that day. He had been asked if he knew or did not know when he went to Oklahoma that a subpoena had been served on him. He said he did not. I knew that he did know. So he was not speaking the truth to the grand jury. So the FBI took out a warrant for his arrest for perjury.
>
> I did not want to be the guy that arrested Murray Humphreys. I had met him so many times that I had a certain regard for him. I didn't want to be there in the moment of his acute embarrassment. So we sent three of our very best agents, most capable, most experienced men, up to Humphreys's apartment on the fifty-first floor of the Marina Building, to arrest him. They announced themselves, shouted very loudly that they were FBI agents and that they had a warrant for his arrest. He refused to open the door. So they announced that they would kick the door down, that they were coming through that door whatever happened. At that point he opened the door and confronted them with a pistol. They could have shot him right there. They had every legal right to do so: they had a warrant for his arrest, he pulled a pistol on them. But they didn't, they refrained, and I

think the reason they refrained was because it was Murray Humphreys. If it had been Sam Giancana, they would probably have been very quick to dispatch him. These agents didn't know Humphreys personally but they knew his image, so they didn't kill him. They wrestled with him and took his gun and went into the apartment, which they had every right to do, and said they were going to conduct a search incidental to the arrest.

Humphreys felt that the FBI agents had to have a search warrant, that the arrest wasn't sufficient in itself. He fought with them. We knew that he had a safe in that apartment and that in the safe he had a black book, and in that black book were the names of all the people he had corrupted, all the public officials, all the judges, all the law-enforcement officers, and their telephone numbers and addresses. We wanted that black book. He, for the same reasons that we wanted it, didn't want us to have it. He had the keys to the safe in his pocket. He put his hand in his pocket. He refused to let the agents have the keys so that they had to rip the pocket off forcibly. It was an emotional situation and a very distressing one for Humphreys. The FBI agents brought him downtown, and he was arraigned and let out on bail of $100,000. Later that evening I saw him on television, where he was as witty and charming as ever. Later that evening I had a phone call and heard that he was dead, of a heart attack, in his apartment.

The body was discovered at 8:30 P.M. by his ever-faithful elder brother, Ernest, who was still helping in the business. The family came up from Oklahoma: his first wife, Mary, daughter Llewella, and her young son George. Humphreys had not wanted any but the family at his funeral, none of the Outfit or its satraps. And so it was, except that they did allow the FBI agent Roemer, of whom he had seen so much, to come to pay his last respects.

The Chicago papers had cleared the front pages to carry the news of the death of one of its sons who, for all his efforts to avoid the light, manifestly figured in the files of the *Tribune*, *Daily News*, and *Sun-Times* more prominently than he could have wanted. The news stories had an heroic ring: "Humphreys

Picked Up Capone's Mantle" the *Daily News* put it, observing:

> Although Humphreys started out as a pistol-packing ruffian,
> he soon found that his brains spoke louder than his muscle.
> Those who met the handsome, soft-spoken, seemingly so well-
> mannered man of recent years found it hard to believe that he
> once was identified as one of the gunmen who shot down seven
> rival gangsters in the 1929 killing that is still known the world
> over as the St. Valentine's Day Massacre. . . . At the time of his
> death Humphreys was still the crime syndicate's master fixer,
> the man who could "reach out for" a judge, a policeman, or
> even a Congressman.

As the news pages offered thousands of words on the Camel's
exploits from his days as a child prodigy of crime, the editorials
showed a higher sense of duty. DEATH OF A "SMART" HOODLUM
was the *Daily News* heading:

> As thugs go, Murray Humphreys was smarter than most. One
> proof of this is the fact that some 32 years after a Chicago police
> official told him to get out of town because his day was done,
> Humphreys was still in town and presumably still plying his
> shadowy trade. . . . Like most gangsters, Humphreys shielded
> his private life from view, which led to a lot of speculation
> about his activities and his income. . . . But it sounds as if the
> one-time successor to Al Capone as Chicago's kingpin gangster
> had made a rather glamorous life for himself over the years. . . .
> It is fitting to wonder, though, how often through the years he
> had sat too frightened to answer a knock on his door, and what
> he would have given for an unconditional release from the
> bondage of his fear.

The *Sun-Times* offered AFFLUENT GUNMAN:

> Murray (The Camel) Humphreys, whose first name was really
> Llewelyn, was a grammar school drop-out before World War I.
> Like many others of his generation he became a self-educated
> success in his field. While other men started at the bottom as
> messengers and clerks and worked their way up to become

executives of business, Humphreys started at the bottom of his field as a burglar and hired gunman and worked to the top in the Crime Syndicate.

On the way Humphreys became a protégé of Al Capone, an associate of some public officials whose sense of ethics was no higher than his own, and he learned to speak drawing room English like an Eliza Dolittle of the underworld. He was a product of our times, of the age of prohibition and the later period of labor racketeering. Although he often moved in respectable circles in his Florida home, virtually he remained a criminal at war with society. Humphreys, like Capone, could exert power and live lavishly only in a society that tolerated him.

The obituaries do not touch on important aspects of Humphreys's later career and especially his role in big business, in laundering money for corporations. The secret, perhaps, had been too well kept. Or was it a matter best left alone?

A week after the Camel's death, the *Daily News* returned to his career in a column by Mike Royko. He wrote:

It wouldn't be right to let Murray Humphreys pass from the scene without mentioning one of his lesser-known but important functions in local affairs. Humphreys was a highly skilled talent scout. According to scholars of such matters, he was the crime syndicates' leading recruiter of young blood, if you'll pardon the expression. He could reach into the backwoods and find a talented machine-gun player in much the same way that George Halas [the football coach] sometimes spots star material in little colleges. . . . Many of the men who developed into outstanding figures owed a debt to their discoverer Humphreys. If the subject of retiring the Camel ever came up, someone surely blubbered, "Gee, but it was Murray who gave me my first break. I was just a nothing—then he let me shoot somebody."

The list of people he discovered, cultivated, taught and helped boost to success reads like an all-star team of undesirables. Humphreys could boast, and probably did, that nobody he ever brought in turned out to be less than a complete slob. In Jasper, Alabama, of all places, he found the fabled Sam (Golf Bag) Hunt. There was Sam, probably running around Jasper barefoot, looking for a turnip to steal, when Humphreys spotted him. He brought Hunt to Chicago and gave him a machine gun and assigned him to the job of keeping people from harming their leader Al Capone. Sam Giancana was little more than an unknown semi-illiterate when Humphreys took him in hand. Today Giancana is a well-known semi-illiterate. His big break came when Humphreys assigned him to a team of messengers, errand boys, drivers, and bodyguards for the wives of Ricca, Campagna, and Gioe who were in federal prison at the time. It was Humphreys who promoted Hyman Gottfried to the role of a courier. He could read a little, which helped him find street addresses.

James (Cat Eyes) Catura had no real direction in life until Humphreys put him to work blowing up people and things. During the thirties, when he was helping the syndicate get into organized labor, he brought along many non-laboring labor leaders such as Joey Glimco, who kept his foot on the throats of Chicago's labor leaders for many years while leading them.

Nobody knows how Humphreys did it. Some people thought that he would rap a prospect on the head and, if he heard a bongo drum sound, he knew he had a recruit. Others said that Humphreys would judge a prospect by his parents. If he had any, he was discarded. There is another theory that his system was no more complicated than turning over a rock and seeing what crawled out.

Mr. Royko's severe judgment was balanced by another appraisal in which we read that the Welshman "devised legal strategies and political fixes that have yet to be equaled. He engendered appreciation for his immense intellect, his finesse and, again within the perspective of his vocation, his civility."

However mixed the panegyrics and however modest his funeral—itself symbolic of his thesis that the mob had to change its ways and follow his quiet example—those colleagues, and the public officials, whether in the law or politics, who had been awed by him in life were to be beguiled by him, too, in death. ARE CRYPTIC FIGURES THE KEY TO CAMEL'S $10 MILLION DOLLAR CACHE? was the headline on an Art Petaque article in the March 1969 *Chicago Sun-Times*. "Investigators," he writes

> have tracked down hundreds of leads and the notation "No 46-400 at 20" still stumps them. It turned up on one of the 17 pages of loose-leaf notes found in Humphreys's 51st floor Marina City apartment by federal agents who arrested the gangster. Could it be a code to the location? . . . An indication of his income can be gauged from the tax case the government prepared against him for the years 1957 to 1962. His known income was $452,111. How much he was able to hide from the government can only be guessed. Immense profits flowed to him from the mob's gambling enterprises. Humphreys reportedly owned a piece of the action at two of the biggest casinos in Las Vegas, Nevada, before he died. . . . Communiqués to Swiss banks and checks with U.S. banks on holders of safe-deposit boxes have failed to turn up a hoard.

And in 1984, Mr. Petaque told me, the money had still not been found. When I asked his daughter about it, she laughed: perhaps it had been "Mr. Moneybags's" last witticism, perpetuating mischief into the hereafter.

If the favorable death notices had about them something of the elegance of Winston Churchill's elegy on the death of his friend, David Lloyd George—"His swift, penetrating, comprehensive mind was always grasping at the root of any question. His eye ranged ahead of the obvious. He was always hunting in the fields beyond"—none raised the question of whether it was necessary for Llewelyn Morris Humphreys to be a gangster. Was it inevitable, some dark force in his nature, or was it mere social and cultural chance that he spent his life in the Outfit? When raised, the question produced responses as mixed as the obituaries.

His daughter Llewella recalls her father saying of the Outfit, once the "shoot-'em-up" Prohibition days were over, that it killed fewer people than supposedly respectable firms did in the normal course of business. And even in the bootlegging days the murders were between, or within, the gangs. But she argues that it is important to remember the period in which he grew up. At the age of seven he was

> on a street corner selling newspapers for a living. And in Chicago, to make the most money you had to have the best corner and you had to get up very early and fight to see who could win the best corner. A bloody nose was not uncommon. He tended to be a bit of a fighter, hot-tempered. My mother told me that once a week she would have to go and fetch him out of jail for fighting. But the truth is that he very often said that he regretted his profession, but that he had made his decision and he had to stick with it. In his young days you either were educated or you went into the Organization. There were no other ways of making money, and he vowed that his family would never do without in the way he had done without. I remember one night when I was in high school, I heard him—he and mother were talking, thinking I was asleep—and he said: "I'm so tired, I want out so bad, but I can't. I have to live with it." That must have been about 1950, and it became worse when the bugging started. The privacy that he had always tried to arrange no longer existed.

FBI agent William Roemer, for all his high regard for Humphreys, or perhaps because of it, would not accept the daughter's appraisal.

> A lot of people grew up in the same neighborhood in the same era, and they didn't turn out to be gangsters and mobsters. I feel just the opposite argument applies to Murray Humphreys. He had a talent and a native intelligence that would have enabled him to do anything. He could have been a success in any aspect of our society. It was a shame that he associated with these animals—because that is what they are, the dregs of society. His

working on their behalf enabled them to be so much more effective and efficient than they would ever have been if it hadn't been for Murray Humphreys.

Mr. Irwin Weiner, however, who was the bondsman who put up the $100,000 bail for Murray Humphreys in the last months of his life, could see no reason why the Welshman should have done other than he did. His admiration for the Camel's courage, elegance, generosity, and talents is complete, his memory still warm. The day I met Mr. Weiner in the Loop in 1983, he was irritated that the Chicago Crime Commission had included his name in a list of members of the Outfit, which he thought unfair; and he was still shaken by witnessing the Teamsters' Union leader, Allen Dorfman, shot dead alongside him recently in a hotel parking lot in the city. He would not accept the agument that the great gangster could have been a fine political leader. "Murray was too truthful, so I don't know how good a politician he would have been since one of the prime requisites of being a politician is not to be truthful."

His tomb stands on a mound in a copse in the long grass of the parkland surrounding the house he built in Oklahoma. His surname alone is carved in the marble; no Christian names. In life the prince saw no reason to attract attention to himself; similarly in death.

16

The Camel's inheritance

Men rage against Materialism, as they call it, forgetting that there has been no material improvement that has not spiritualized the world, and that there have been few, if any, spiritual awakenings that have not wasted the world's faculties in barren hopes, and fruitless aspirations, and empty or trammeling creeds. What is termed Sin is an essential element of progress. Without it the world would stagnate, or grow old, or become colorless. By its curiosity Sin increases the experience of the race. Through its intensified assertion of individualism, it saves us from the monotony of type. In its rejection of the current notions about morality, it is one with the higher ethics.

—Oscar Wilde

The hand that signed the paper felled city;
Five sovereign fingers taxed the breath,
Doubled the globe of dead and halved a country;
These five kings did a king to death . . .

—Dylan Thomas,
Twenty-Five Poems, 1936

Just as every immigrant group in the United States, whether of European, South American, or Asian origin, will feel the nation belongs to them, so most foreigners have their own America in mind. Any judgment of Llewelyn Morris Humphreys's career and achievement will be colored by the palette it is painted from. Fugitive and cloistered minds will regard him as yet another demonstration that the United States is corrupt. Such extremism is not helpful in gauging the insidiousness of Humphreys's insights and capacity.

Knowing about Murray Humphreys demonstrates how the melodramatic representation of the Mafia in *The Godfather* distracted attention from a more serious corruption. Why should it not still be doing so? When the mob or Outfit or Syndicate is presented as gaudy, peopled by easily recognized members of a particular race, its members can be isolated as an apparent aberration in a society. Identify a Capone, or any of his less celebrated successors, and you have a dangerous yet comfortable idea: these are hoodlums beyond the pale. Concentrate on their peculiar loyalties and savage customs, persuade yourself that they kill within the circles of their sodality, and the respectable world, if not altogether safe from the stray bullet, is formally inviolate. To say of that man sitting across the bar or restaurant that he is a member of the Outfit, as one might say he's a famous actor or writer, is more agreeable than having to wonder if the lawyer or businessman or politician who is in your company derives his income from a more mysterious manifestation of that same mob.

Given that Humphreys was at all successful in seeing to it that gangster funds went into respectable commercial enterprises—and his talent at everything else he turned his hand to would suggest so—any sentient man in American commercial life is in an odd position. Either he doesn't know if the Outfit's money supports his enterprise and worries, or he does know and worries. Not every businessman, of course, is sentient so that many may consider the matter nonsense. It's common gossip in most of the world's financial centers, London as much as Tokyo, that Mafia money is coming into town. Who wants it? The prospect is more taxing when it is Mafia money arriving without anyone's knowing that it is such, but traveling incognito, as Humphreys traveled.

In the past, in America, bold spirits who have shared Oscar Wilde's opinion, that without sin the "world would stagnate, or grow old, or become colorless," have agreed with him that it intensifies individualism. Wilde may have been frivolous; those who adored the buccaneering antics of the robber barons, the Fisks and Goulds, the Rockefellers and Vanderbilts, J. P. Morgan and Carnegie; or the skulduggery of Insull and Yerkes; or the flamboyance of Colosimo and Capone, of Hinky Dink and the Bath, were being serious. This was the vigor of the New World, creating and stealing wealth, the stuff of a wild new society where everything goes. Sin it may be—and, true, many suffer—but it's fun.

This cheerful rejoicing in wickedness is no longer heard. But the drive of the robber barons remains the society's main engine. If Wilde is right, material improvement has been spiritualized in the United States. That passion to make money, the desire to win, is assumed to be a necessary condition of a democratic society.

Let's suppose, then, that the worship of Mammon is the spiritual fuel in the American engine, that it really has come a long way from Pennsylvania, not to mention Virginia, from Thomas Jefferson and the Adams family, or Boston's grand families who spoke only to God. How much does it matter if such a society is corrupted? When Humphreys held his long sway, how much was the citizen troubled when, shall we say, he sat on a jury and heard the suave Welshman win an acquittal, to the fury of the prosecution? Did the jury member know that the judge might have been bought, that the prosecuting lawyer was a stooge, that the police were fixed? If he did, or did not, how seriously did he reflect on the noble aspirations of his Constitution? When a manager in an insurance or construction company discovered that honest business could not be done because the Outfit had an arrangement with City Hall, how disturbed was his faith in the nature of his democracy? These would be relatively tranquil disturbances contrasted with the violent intrusions of the mob's men at your place of work or your apartment or neighborhood bar, but more troubling perhaps if you took your nation's pretensions solemnly.

Most of us in our own professions are aware of the debilitating effect of minor corruption, mostly taking the form of the fiddling of expenses or hours of work. When a conspiracy exists whereby it is generally known in an enterprise that the board of directors, managers, staff, or workers, are all involved, then it may seem, even if illegal, an agreeable arrangement. What can be wrong, when everyone is doing it? Yet it seems to create, even among people who might boast about their tricks, a general unease, a shiftiness, as if some deep moral seam is being touched, indefinable, half-forgotten when discernible. And so the quality of work and enthusiasm for a skill is diminished. If that happens on so commonplace a level, what reason is there to suppose that the effect is different in a grander, more sonorous context?

Humphreys worked on the assumption that every man had his price, and unfortunately never saw any evidence, among the wide range of prominent fellow citizens he dealt with, ever to change his analysis. It could be that he was careful not to approach people who knew the value rather than the price of selling themselves, or is that a generous cavil? His cynicism is shared by many. That everyone is on the take is a general assumption. And yet there remains, as Lloyd George observed, that vague desire to aspire to something higher in the life of the whole society. President Nixon, after all, did fall from power— even if his fall took a long time and is still thought by many of his fellows to be an unnecessarily harsh consequence of behavior that was scarcely all that unusual. This surely demonstrates a public desire for proper behavior. It also shows that Richard Nixon, one of the most experienced of American politicians, saw nothing wrong in what he did.

If corruption matters in a society it is because a democratic leadership needs to make demands on its people, such as conscripting them for war, which may be easy in a totalitarian state but can be met with hostility or indifference if the people do not trust the leaders making the demands. The dreadful behavior of

U.S. conscripts in Vietnam was a brutal consequence. If this is a potential problem in a small society, how much more so in a huge federal empire where the character of the population changes endlessly? The wild effect of Chicago on an older American tradition was dramatic; the incursion of South Americans and Asians will further dilute the language of an old puritanism. If citizens grow skeptical about the legality of authority, and government wishes to preserve its power, its logic will become more authoritarian. Not a pretty thought. The old rhetoric remains (Mammon and the going for gold not lending themselves to more than hucksterism and hype), but wears thinner.

The happy thought is that there cannot anymore be a Humphreys in American life, that he was a historical accident, born perfectly in his time. No more will a man move easily among political leaders, judges, lawyers, trade union leaders, and businessmen of all kinds, actors and singers—and, above all, gangster colleagues—persuading all to his will and carrying in his pocket not only votes and money-bribes but a threat of death. Yet there was once a belief that the sinister days of crime had ended with Capone, that it was an unfortunate consequence of Prohibition alone.

How can we be sure there is no Humphreys now? He evaded attention most of his lifetime. It is hard to believe that any successor would possess all his gifts and especially not the wry, laconic manner in which he held up a slightly distorted mirror to the formal goals of American society. Moneybags, the brainy Welsh hood, Curly, the Hump—the Camel was, as his fellow Chicagoans recognized, the "boldest of them all," unique in his murderous community. However, there may be lesser men, achieving not so much but carrying forward the tradition he established of a fruitful relationship between law and crime, between the elected representatives of the people and the laundering of dishonest gain. Even without a successor, his inheritance would insure that the "disease" so cogently diagnosed by Machiavelli so long ago remains virulent enough to disturb any sanguine view of the world's most powerful nation.

Cast and glossary

ACCARDO, ANTHONY JOSEPH.
A bodyguard for Al Capone and a suspect in the St. Valentine's Day Massacre, who was employed by Humphreys or, rather, paid a salary by Humphreys in the brewery and laundry business. After Humphreys's death in 1965, Accardo, who had been arrested at least thirty times on charges as varied as murder, extortion, and tax evasion, assumed control of the Outfit.

AIUPPA, JOSEPH.
A minor gangster in Humphreys's time, who became an important ally of Accardo when the Welshman died.

ALEX, GUS.
An important ally of Humphreys in the Loop, particularly in his work among politicians, trade union leaders, lawyers, and gamblers. A familiar suspect in murder and bribery cases.

BIOFF, WILLIAM.
In the late thirties the union leader who, under Humphreys's instruction, corrupted Hollywood, but would not name the Welshman in evidence that sent Ricca, Nitti, Fischetti, and Campagna to jail. Later Bioff was murdered.

CAMPAGNA, LOUIS.
An expert marksman. Brought in as an assassin by Capone; known as "Little New York." Humphreys was to use him after

Capone's death to support whoever was at the head of the Outfit or the Mafia.

CAPONE, ALPHONSE.

Capone, the most famous of gangsters who depended on Humphreys's talent toward the end of the twenties, was also known as Scarface, Little Caesar, or Big Al. While his political judgment was often poor, his control of his own troops was complete. Mysteriously, Humphreys seems to have done nothing to have Capone removed from prison, even though exercising ingenuity to bring about the parole of others. Probably the task was too much although this failure did increase Humphreys's power.

CERMAK, ANTON.

A Democratic politician in Chicago who was assassinated while he was mayor in 1933, standing alongside the newly elected Democratic president, Franklin D. Roosevelt. He was elected mayor in the belief that he was an enemy of crime. This was a misapprehension. He had his own gang in mind. This was probably why he was shot, leading to a view that no one in fact wanted to shoot the president. Cermak was the target.

COLOSIMO, JAMES.

Known as Big Jim. He began a career as a street sweeper at the turn of the century, married a brothel owner, and grew rich in the white slave and gambling trades. His restaurant attracted Caruso, Galli-Curci, Tetrazzini, and John McCormack. He probably set the tone for twentieth-century Chicago crime. He proves one point; an acolyte murdered him when Prohibition began, so the tradition existed before bootlegging.

COUGHLIN, JOHN.

Known as Bath House or The Bath. Coughlin exploited his proprietorship of the bathhouse he owned as a source of votes. His Irish Catholic connections established his power. He gave memorable parties. His influence diminished in the twenties when Capone pursued a more maverick policy and even abandoned the Bath's Democrats for the Republicans.

DALEY, RICHARD.

Known as "the Boss," he insured in the fifties and sixties that the Democratic machine, built up by Hinky Dink, the Bath, Cermak, Kelly, and Nash, kept control of the city and of Cook County, the territory of greater Chicago. He suffered from scandals but survived them. He kept his distance from Humphreys, which did not diminish the influence of the Outfit, particularly in the election of President Kennedy.

DARROW, CLARENCE.

One of the most eloquent of American lawyers, whose heroic defense of radical trade union leaders in violent times at the turn of the century was followed by his defense of others who were gangsters of Humphreys's acquaintance.

DELUCIA, PAUL.

Better known as Paul (The Waiter) Ricca. A great fan of Humphreys although a senior Mafia figure. He was always impressed by the Welshman's capacity to settle matters with the authorities.

EISENHOWER, DWIGHT D.

The Commander-in-Chief of American and Allied Forces in Europe in World War II, who became Republican President from 1952 to 1960. That he should have met Humphreys and his fellow gangsters in Chicago might seem surprising—except that in Chicago politics, surprise is an impossible concept.

FISCHETTI, CHARLES.

A relative of Al Capone's who was very useful to Humphreys in developing gambling in Las Vegas. He later was to be irritating to "The Camel" by encouraging Sam Giancana in his relationship with the CIA over Cuba and Castro.

GIANCANA, SAM.
A busy gunman in his youth and protege of Humphreys. He became the formal head of the Outfit in the late fifties. He loved the limelight. He became involved in plots to recapture Cuba or kill Castro. (Humphreys is thought to have disapproved of this, and certainly he seems to have made no effort to keep Giancana out of jail.) He was probably murdered by colleagues.

GLIMCO, JOSEPH.
An ally of Humphreys in organizing trade unions in Chicago, particularly the Teamsters Union, of which another Humphreys protege, James Hoffa, became president.

GUZIK, JAKE.
Al Capone's accountant, a man who tried to avoid violence but was not always successful. He became an ally of Humphreys, whose wife, Mary, was to help Guzik with the accounts. Like the Camel, he was a survivor and, like all survivors, was held to be wise.

KENNA, MICHAEL.
Known as Hinky-Dink because he was a small and cheerful man of Irish descent. He became, with his friend the Bath, the controller of the Loop. Although remembered for the style in which he brought corruption in Chicago to a standard unknown before the First World War, his defenders argue that he made the lives of the new immigrants less miserable than they would have been otherwise. Hinky-Dink had style.

THE KENNEDYS.
The father of this important American Catholic family, Joe, was a rival of Humphreys in the bootlegging battles. His son John became President of the United States in 1960 and was murdered in 1963. Another son, Robert, became Attorney General in his brother's administration and was murdered in 1968. The Attorney General became a passionate prosecutor of Humphreys and his fellow mobsters.

LEVEE.

That part of downtown Chicago that, toward the end of the last century and the beginning of this one, offered brothels and gambling dens of a disrepute and elegance the world had not before seen. What fascinated the visitor was that so much activity went on within shooting distance of the palaces of the rich, the new commercial skyscrapers, and the hovels of the new immigrants. When the Levee was cleaned up a little, it became known as the Loop.

LIBONATI, ROLAND V.

Chicago lawyer who served first in the Illinois Congress and later in Washington. Humphreys was arrested at the Congressman's first election victory party when all the gangsters placed their guns on the piano. He acted as Humphreys's defense counsel from time to time, met him frequently in Washington, and helped argue the case for the parole of such of the Camel's colleagues unfortunate enough to be in jail. Mr. Libonati speaks well of Humphreys and assures the author of his—Libonati's— ignorance of crime in Chicago.

THE LOOP.

The heart of Chicago's commercial and political wealth takes its name from the elevated railroad that winds between its buildings. The Loop incorporates, as the Levee did, the First Ward, which was to be the political stronghold of Humphreys and his precursors, Hinky-Dink and Bath House.

MCGURN.

Known as Machine Gun Jack and one of the most reckless of killers employed by Capone. Once tried to kill the entertainer Joe E. Lewis, because he had been offered a contract with a nightclub in Chicago other than the one controlled by the Outfit. Capone apologized and paid for the operation to restore the singer's vocal cords.

MORAN, BUGS.

A friend of Dion O'Banion. Sometimes an ally and sometimes a rival of Al Capone's. It was Moran's attempt to play a joke on the Capone mob that is held to have produced the St. Valentine's Day Massacre in 1929.

NITTI, FRANK.

Known as The Enforcer. He was a necessary murderer for Capone and was Humphreys's principal ally when Capone went to jail. Nitti killed himself rather than go to prison in the Hollywood corruption scandal. This unique suicide might have been due to Nitti's distress that his wife had died young.

O'BANION, DION.

The leader of the Irish mobs, a former altar boy who abandoned ambitions for the Catholic priesthood and instead became one of Chicago's most notorious murderers. When he attempted to seize power, the Capone mob killed him and so insured its triumph. Humphreys, who began his career like O'Banion, selling newspapers, is thought to have found the Irishman's fate instructive.

SIEGEL, BENJAMIN.

Known as Bugsy, he cooperated with Humphreys in arranging for the legalization of gambling in Nevada with Meyer Lansky and Sam Giancana, and later began setting up casinos in the Caribbean and Middle East. He fell out with the Mafia over a deal in Las Vegas. They murdered him.

STEVENSON, ADLAI.

Governor of Illinois and the nominee of the Democratic party for the Presidency in 1952 and 1956. A member of the Chicago Democratic machine, although his worldwide repute was that of a high-minded liberal wit. He lost both elections to General Eisenhower and failed to win the Democratic nomination in 1960, partly because Mayor Daley decided to abandon him for Senator John F. Kennedy, whose subsequent narrow victory Chicago notoriously arranged.

THOMPSON, WILLIAM.

Known as Big Bill. A Republican, he won three elections as Mayor of Chicago. He was a super American patriot, sportsman, and clown. He personified the braggadocio Chicagoans often fell for. One year he was for the gangs, another year against them; but he always won their support until, in the end, the Democrats pulled themselves together and upset him in 1931. His successor, Anton Cermak, was assassinated.

TORRIO, JOHN.

Brought in by Big Jim Colosimo to handle his affairs, he is suspected of murdering his patron. Torrio organized Chicago to meet the challenge of Prohibition. In turn he brought in Al Capone from New York, but soon found that his protege's dynamism fractured the cool steel of the Torrio approach. Torrio, like Humphreys later, saw no reason for indiscriminate violence. Capone's antics and the warfare that led to Torrio's almost being murdered persuaded him to return to the more peaceful life of crime in New York.

TUOHY, ROGER.

A minor but successful bootlegger in the twenties. Tuohy joined the Democratic campaign of Mayor Cermak. Believed to have been framed (for kidnapping) by Humphreys, he spent twenty-five years in jail. When he was released in 1959, he was murdered in Chicago after publishing his autobiography. Humphreys's alibi is considered a classic (see Chapter 13).

WEINSHANK, AL.

Until the arrival of Humphreys in the laundry business, Weinshank was one of the most important trade union figures in Chicago. He joined Bugs Moran's gang and was murdered in the St. Valentine's Day Massacre.

Bibliography

Allsop, Kenneth. *The Bootleggers*. New York: Doubleday, 1961.

Brashler, William. *The Don: the Life and Death of Sam Giancana*. New York: Harper & Row, 1977.

Boyer, Richard O., and Morais, Herbert M. *A History of the American Labour Movement*. London: John Calder, 1955.

Dedmon, Emmett. *Fabulous Chicago*. New York: Random House, 1953.

Demaris, Ovid. *Captive City*. New York: Lyle Stuart, 1969.

Giancana, Antoinette and Renner, Thomas C. *Mafia Princess*. New York: William Morrow, 1984.

Hecht, Ben. *A Child of the Century*. New York: Simon and Schuster, 1954.

———. *Charlie*. New York: Harper & Brothers, 1957.

Jones, Eirwen. *Folk Tales of Wales*. London: Thomas Nelson, 1947.

Jones, Gwyn (ed). *The Oxford Book of Welsh Verse in English*. Oxford University Press, 1977.

Kefauver, Estes. *Crime in America*. New York: Doubleday, 1951.

Kobler, John. *Capone*. New York: Putnam's, 1971.

Lerner, Max. *The Unfinished Country*. New York: Simon and Schuster, 1959.

Machiavelli, Niccolò. (Translated by Peter Bondonella and Mark Musa). *The Prince*. Oxford University Press, 1984.

Morgan, Kenneth O. *Rebirth of a Nation: Wales 1880-1980*.

Oxford: Clarendon Press, 1981.

Pasley, Fred D. *Al Capone: the Biography of a Self-Made Man.* London: Faber, 1931.

Peterson, Virgil W. *Barbarians in our Midst.* Boston: Little, Brown, 1952.

Rees, Goronwy. *The Great Slump.* London: Weidenfeld & Nicolson, 1970.

Royko, Mike. *Boss: Mayor Richard J. Daley of Chicago.* New York: Dutton, 1971.

Shannon, William V. *The Heir Apparent: Robert Kennedy and the Struggle for Power.* New York: Macmillan, 1967.

Thomas, Bob. *King Cohn.* New York: Putnam, 1967.

Thomas, Brinley. *Migration and Economic Growth.* Cambridge University Press, 1954.

Terkel, Studs. *Division Street: America.* New York: Pantheon, 1966.

Touhy, Roger. *The Stolen Years.* New York: Pennington, 1959.

Williams, Gwyn A. *The Welsh in Their History.* London: Croom Helm, 1982.

Wilson, Edmund. *The American Earthquake.* New York: Doubleday, 1958.

Index